The Answer:

The Road to Peace

A Book That Was Prophesied Prior to Her Birth

R. S. Kurtz

ISBN: 978-0-9787652-6-2

Library of Congress Control Number: 2012922310

Dove image credit: The Stock Exchange image uploaded
by voodoo4u2n

Pathway image credit: The Stock Exchange image
uploaded by josecarli

FOREWORD

❦

Every human life has a unique story, but only a few people "put pen to paper." I'm glad that Rose Kurtz has written a candid and inspiring story about her life of more than 80 years. Its significance actually began with a dream her mother had not long before Rose was born. Her book is the story of a little Jewish girl with a spiritual nature and inquisitive mind who grew up to have broad beliefs and be a significant "giver" to the world.

Though Rose is a practical person, she has always had a rich inner life, too. She wondered as a child, "If there is one God, why do we have so many religions?" Like Mohandas Gandhi, she was a shy child who listened intently to all around her. She pondered deep questions while, with a good spirit, she met her life challenges.

Denied college by her mother, Rose became successful in business while married and raising 4 sons. Later, when taking business courses in college, she was confronted by this question, "How do you want to be remembered after you're gone?" Pondering that question completely altered the direction of her life and she changed her major to become a social worker, specifically to work with the aged. Always plucky, she incorporated, with others, a non-profit group called ALLY, which means "people working together for a common cause." The initials actually stand for Alternative Living for Later Years, and the group did much creative work for the elderly.

Rose says that a Dr. Martin Luther King, Jr. quote says it all, "An individual has not started living until he can rise above the narrow confines of his individualistic concerns to the broader concerns of all humanity." Another of her quotes comes from the great Dr. Albert Schweitzer (my first peace hero) who said, "One thing I know: the only ones among you who will be really happy are those who have sought and found how to serve."

She also quotes others, such as Dr. Alfred Adler, on overcoming childhood insecurity. He said there are two ways to overcome these feelings. One way is to strive for success by working for the betterment of mankind. The second way is to strive for superiority. The latter approach is not considered healthy since it only focuses on personal achievement.

Another quote is from Ken Keyes, Jr. who says in *The Power of Unconditional Love*, "The social cooperativeness that flows when we love everyone as a brother or sister is needed to help solve the immense planetary problems we have created."

There are hints of mysticism in her story, such as when she and her guests heard the chirping of a bird inside her home. Later she learned that her beloved sister had passed at that time.

The last half of the book includes practical advice on how to overcome feelings of inferiority (which most people have), how to take care of our bodies and emotions, and hints on how to age successfully.

Woven into this half are her convictions. She believes "It's not important how long we live but what we do with the years we are given. Live life to the fullest and give as much as possible to others. This is what lives on when we are gone." When once asked what she would like her epitaph to be, she thought and decided, "She made the world just a little bit better." Indeed she did—and still is doing, with this inspiring story of her life!

Did she ever receive the answer to her childhood question? Not exactly. She investigated several religions over the years and accepts them all. The great Mahatma Gandhi said, "Like the bee gathering honey from the different flowers, the wise person accepts the essence of the different scriptures, and sees only the good in all religions." However, Rose is particularly drawn to the Baha'i religion, which believes we are approaching the beginning of "The Most Great Peace." Would that this be so! Baha'i is not my faith, but I honor her choice.

So what is peace, and how can it be achieved? Rose says, "Peace cannot be achieved by the dictates of one country or one world leader. It must come about through the consciousness of multitudes of men and women who have first loved themselves, and then extended this love to the balance of mankind."

Rose's bright spirit and lack of ego drew me deeply into her story. It has inspired me to write about my life, and perhaps you will do the same!

—Christine Dull

Co-Founder

Dayton International Peace Museum

INTRODUCTION

❦

This book is the story of my spiritual journey through the early years of my life, and how I ultimately found and accepted the Baha'i Faith. But the story is for people of all faiths and creeds who yearn for peace. Each religion recognizes the need for love, brotherhood and harmony in our lives. Now, as we go through the twenty-first century, it is time for all people to reach out to our sisters and brothers, and project their love to the worldwide community—all nations, all religions, all cultures. Indeed, we are all one people. We are the human race. Somewhere inside, no matter what your religion calls God, you are aware that it is His Divine Will to promote peace throughout the entire planet earth. Join us as we make this trip together along the road to peace.

CHAPTER ONE

❧❧

Her high-pitched scream tore through the quiet night air like a bullet racing to reach its mark.

Sam Marsden bolted to an upright position in bed. Lying next to him was Anna, his wife of twelve years. Sam looked down at Anna who was lying flat on her back. Her abdomen was distended to huge proportions as her due date was fast approaching. In just a few weeks she was scheduled to deliver her fourth child. The Marsden family now includes Eleanor, 10, Bernard, 9, and Clara who was on the brink of her seventh birthday.

Sam got out of bed and informed his mate who was now wide awake, "I'd better see what's wrong. I'll bet Clara is having another one of her nightmares."

He walked across the hall and opened the door where the two girls shared a bedroom. Clara was sitting on the edge of her bed. She was trying to stifle the sobs which were convulsing through her tiny body. As her father appeared, she blurted out between sobs, "It happened again. There was a big fire. It was terrible, Daddy. Everything was burning and I couldn't do anything about it."

Sam walked over to his frightened daughter. He hugged her and tried to comfort her. "Everything's all right now. There is no fire. It was just a dream."

After a pause, Clara continued, "I know it was a dream. Why do I keep having the same dream? It scares me so much. I don't want to see the fire again!! Daddy, why is this happening to me?"

Sam had no answer for his young daughter. This was the third time in a month she had dreamed about a fire. He was concerned about these ongoing dreams, and he wished he had a better answer to give. He tried to quiet her as he said, "I can't explain why you're having this terrible dream. But everything is OK. There is no fire. Try to go back to sleep." Then he tucked her back into bed and gave her a gentle kiss on her forehead.

Sam Marsden was not a tall man. He was only five foot five, but he had the heart of a giant. He loved his wife and children dearly, and showered much affection on them. His head was crowned with pitch black hair, and his frame was fairly lean. On his chin was a birthmark, deep purple in color, but his children who saw him every day barely noticed it. Clara, comforted by her father's presence, closed her eyes and soon went back to sleep.

It was June 1931, and the United States was in the throes of the Great Depression. Sam who had come to this country from Russia as a teenager had very little formal education. He worked in a brass foundry where he was doing manual labor to support his family. It was very hot in the foundry, and he spent many hours doing the heavy lifting which his job required. Ann tried to help by working as a seamstress when work was available. They had managed to put aside enough money to buy a house in the Cobbs Creek section of Philadelphia. The house was directly across from Cobbs Creek Park, and the family was delighted with the vast expanse of grass where the children could run and play.

By the following week the children had finished their semesters in school and were happily looking forward to their summer vacations. They were all good students, but it was nice for them to be able to relax and not be concerned about homework and tests. In order to celebrate their good grades and the start of the summer vacation Sam said, "How would you like to go to a movie tonight?"

His question was met by an enthusiastic response. "Oh, Dad, that's great. The movie is air-conditioned, and it will feel great to get away from this heat," said Elie.

"Could we eat dinner out, before we go to the movie? Horn and Hardart is close by, and it doesn't cost too much," implored Bernie.

Clara turned to her dad and asked, "Is Mommy coming, too?"

Sam shook his head and said, "I'm not sure. Let's ask her."

The four of them walked into the kitchen where Anna was putting away the luncheon dishes. Sam announced his plans for the evening. Then he said, "How about coming along with us? It'll be a nice night out. Once the baby comes, we won't be able to go out very much."

Ann thought about the bus ride and the steep steps of the elevated line which had to be climbed at Sixty-third Street. "No. I don't think so. I think I'll just stay here."

Sam wasn't pleased with her answer. "Are you sure? We don't do too many things together."

Clara chimed in, "Mom, you have to come with us. I don't want you to stay home all by yourself."

"I don't really want to go. It's so hot outside, and I'm going to have the baby any day. I feel so tired. I'd rather stay home and rest."

"Please, Mom," Clara pleaded. "We want you to go with us. You have to come."

Due to Clara's persistence, Ann gave in and agreed to go. That evening the five of them waited for the bus and got off at Market Street where they changed to the Frankford Street Elevated Line. It was a struggle for Anna to climb the steps leading to the

10

loading platform, and she paused twice to gather her energy. In a few minutes the train arrived, and the family boarded and found a seat for Anna. They got off at Fifty-second Street and climbed down the steps. Horn and Hardart cafeteria was right on the corner. The chain was well-known on the East Coast and this was one of their busiest sites.

Anna and Sam picked up their trays and walked along the rail to select their food. The children followed closely behind. The sight of all the food choices was mind-boggling. There was turkey, roast beef, fish, and many more mouth-watering dishes, as well as over a dozen different vegetables to complement the main dish. For once, Ann could sit and enjoy a meal that was prepared by someone else. Money was scarce in their household, and having dinner out was a treat not often enjoyed by the family.

After dinner they took the short walk to Chestnut Street where the theatre was located. Sam purchased the necessary tickets, and they went in and took their seats. Before the main feature started, there were other presentations: the news, coming attractions, a short subject, and a cartoon put out by Disney Studios. Finally, the main feature, City Lights, came on screen. This film is believed by many to be one of Charlie Chaplin's greatest films. There was a complete musical soundtrack and various sound effects. However, there was no speech or dialogue even though it was made three years after the start of the talkies era. Chaplin preferred the silent art form.

The family enjoyed the show, and when it ended, they made the return trip home. As Sam got off the bus, he helped his wife down the steps. In an instant they were both aware of the emergency vehicles parked in front of their house. There were several fire engines with hoses outstretched, and water was being trained on the house. Black puffs of smoke drifted out of the windows which had been broken out by the firemen.

"Oh, my God! Our house is on fire!!" shrieked Anna.

At this point the fire was under control, but the firemen were busy mopping up the hot spots. Once ignited, the fire had raced quickly through the building. There was major damage to the house and its contents. Almost nothing of value could be saved. The investigation which followed showed the fire was electrical in nature.

The couple and their children spent the night with relatives. The next morning they started searching for another place to live. Unfortunately, the fire insurance that was on the property was inadequate to let them rebuild. Once they realized they would not be able to rebuild the house, they searched for a home they could rent. It is devastating to know that the lovely home they had shared was now gone. However after searching for a few weeks they were able to find a small rental property in North Philadelphia which was affordable. They moved in, and with the help of friends and relatives, they were able to make it livable. They would be able to pick up their life and go on.

Two weeks later, Anna went into labor. She entered the hospital, and within a few hours she gave birth to a healthy baby girl. I was that baby girl. My parents named me Rose. Since the recession was still going strong, and the family had just lost its beautiful home, there was not much to celebrate as I came home. But after all, we were all alive and well, and that is the greatest blessing of all.

Following the fire which had destroyed our home, my family's attention was focused on Clara. Her multiple dreams of fire...had eerily come to fruition. The house had been so quickly engulfed by flames, it was possible, if not probable, that my mother, pregnant with me, may not have escaped if she had remained behind as she wanted. Clara's insistence that mom should leave and go to the movie was looked at as something of a miracle. Had my mother been left alone, she could easily have been injured, or overcome by smoke, or worse. Clara's uncanny ability to foresee the future, became a legend. From that time on, she was thought of as our Guardian Angel.

CHAPTER TWO

I don't remember much about my early childhood. I vaguely remember the small row house we lived in.

It was in a section of Philadelphia called Strawberry Mansion. Our home consisted of three bedrooms and one bath, standard fare back in those days. There was a nice open porch enclosed by a wooden railing where I spent much of my time watching the goings-on of the street.

My dad continued to work in the brass foundry until a major medical problem hit home. He developed a large kidney stone, and in removing the stone doctors had to remove his entire kidney. To have only one kidney during the 1930s was a very formidable event. Dad was told he would have to find work that did not involve any strenuous physical labor.

My parents decided to venture into business, and bought a candy store which had living quarters attached. This would be my home for the next fourteen years. At the time we moved in, the neighborhood was "changing," which meant the white residents were leaving and were being replaced by people of color. This was important to my development because these were my friends and playmates. In future years I was extremely agitated and frustrated when I came into contact with someone who was prejudiced. Racism was something I could not understand. The children I played with were like children everywhere. We played games and had fun, and we liked each other never noticing the different skin colors.

Our house had just the basic necessities. Directly in back of the store there was a large room which we used as a dining room. There was a large round table made of mahogany and six upholstered chairs. Against one wall was positioned a matching china cabinet in which Mom kept her good china— used mainly for company. The walls were adorned with heavy, vinyl wallpaper which featured large ivory flowers on a wine-colored background. It certainly didn't add anything to the lack of warmth in the room.

The kitchen was up one step. It was a tiny room, but adequate for our needs. Mom faithfully prepared three meals a day for her family, day after day, and week after week. She was definitely a good cook, and we all enjoyed the Jewish style food that was served to us. Upstairs were three bedrooms and an old-fashioned bathroom. The bathroom served double duty. In addition to serving all of the family's personal needs, my mother washed our laundry in the bathtub, on a regular basis. I can close my eyes and still see Mom kneeling on the floor, bending over the tub, using the scrubbing board to clean each individual piece of laundry. It was many years before we were able to afford a washer and dryer. But being quite young, I didn't have the foggiest idea how difficult it must have been to do all this work by hand. I certainly had no appreciation of all her hard work. It blows my mind today to think of all the arduous hours involved in this task which everyone seemed to take for granted.

The store itself was a "mom and pop" candy store, something that doesn't exist today. Most "mom and pop" stores including grocery stores, have become obsolete as large chain stores with their mass marketing and discounted merchandise evolved on the horizon. In the 1930s the income from our store provided a nice living for my parents who were raising four children at a time when the cost of living was quite low.

During the early years Dad worked really long hours. He opened the store at seven A.M. and closed at eleven P.M. And the store was open seven days a week. That's a lot of hours. Yet, I never heard Dad complain about anything. He was an ideal dad— warm, loving, and very easy-going. If he didn't have this laid-back temperament, he never would have survived with my mom, who was the exact opposite.

Unfortunately, Mom was hard to please and very opinionated. If she said something, that was it! It was either her way, or no way. We all walked on eggshells, and tried not to displease her. She never hit any of us, but she made it clear, that if she said something, we were expected to listen. And it would have been futile to challenge her. On top of this negative aspect of her personality, she was quite cold and distant to all of us. If she was upset with you, she wouldn't speak to you for days. If it weren't for my dad, life in this household would have been unbearable. Mom did work hard to care for all of us, as I stated earlier, and I realize now she just lived life to the best of her ability.

When I needed love and support, I only had to walk the few steps to the store, and Dad would impart all the warmth and nurturing that a growing child yearned for. Needless to say, I spent many hours in the store. Dad had a great sense of humor, and a wonderful way with people. Little did I know that the endless chain of time spent observing my dad interacting with his customers, would be a valuable educational tool, and would become my cornerstone in future years, when I would go on to become a social worker. Dad interacted cordially and effortlessly with people of all ages and with diverse personalities. Even when someone became angry, he stayed very calm, and was able to diffuse the situation by his low-key approach. Who needs school? My father was my best instructor by far. What I learned from him helped me to deal with people and situations throughout my adult life.

CHAPTER THREE

❧❧

The elementary school I attended was only a block away, an easy walk from my home. I always enjoyed school. Today, I guess I would be referred to as a nerd. When I came home from school, I would happily do my homework, and then read whatever I could get my hands on. So, let's face it, I was a nerd. I guess there are worse things to be. At a young age I got a library card, and visited the library often, coming home loaded down with enough reading material to last for a couple of weeks.

Life was fairly uneventful during those first years in West Philadelphia. There were only a few exceptions that stand out in my mind. The first event was really exciting to the entire Marsden household.

Dad was able to save up enough money to purchase a new Ford automobile. The long, sleek, black car with its running board was parked alongside the side entrance to our store. Whenever I looked at it, I was filled with pride. I definitely felt as if I was living in the lap of luxury. Imagine having a car! Although the prices of cars were becoming affordable, it was still considered a great treat to go somewhere by car, rather than traveling by bus or trolley.

The second memorable event wasn't as pleasant. It came about when I was around seven years old. At that time medical wisdom dictated that all young children would be well served by having their tonsils removed. Therefore, a tonsillectomy was scheduled with an ear, nose, and throat specialist. At the appointed time I was driven to the doctor's office, and the surgery took place.

The doctor said that to assist with the healing process, only soft foods such as Jell-O and ice cream should be ingested during the next few days. I was really in luck! The front of our store held a large, stainless steel fixture, which housed Breyer's ice cream in just about every imaginable flavor. For five cents our customers were able to purchase a dip of their favorite ice cream on their choice of a regular cone, or a sugar cone. I never realized how lucky I was to have this great treat available to me on an ongoing basis. Now it was an important item in treating my very sore throat. I could eat all the ice cream I wanted! I preferred my ice cream in a dish, so over the next few days I carried my bowl to the store where it was refilled many times. The coolness of this delicious treat felt so soothing as it slid down my painful throat. This was a child's dream, and I knew I was fortunate to have access to this popular food so readily available.

Three days after my surgery all appeared to be going well. It was late morning when I found myself in my room, sitting at my desk. Upon feeling my nose run, I reached for a tissue and wiped my nose. When I looked at the tissue, I was startled to find it was full of blood. As the bleeding continued, I went downstairs to inform Mom. Applying pressure did not stop the bleeding, and shortly thereafter Mom called the doctor, who asked to see me in his office.

Dad loaded me into the car and made the trip to the doctor's Pine Street office. The rest of the day is somewhat of a blur. I remember the doctor packing my nose, and doing other things generally accepted as a remedy for the situation. He was able to stop the bleeding several times. Unfortunately, the bleeding returned each time, and the process was repeated many times. Toward evening the doctor felt the problem was under control and sent me home. I can vividly recall that as we approached our home I could feel the bleeding begin again. My heart sank as I told Dad what was happening. We went to the doctor's office one more time. My last memory of that day was being tucked into bed by my father. The frightening ordeal had ended, and I was once again safe. However, the question of what caused this episode would hang over me for many years.

Following the tonsillectomy I began to run a low-grade fever. The fever plus the fact that I had a heart murmur led to the diagnosis of rheumatic heart disease. Much to my dismay, I missed several months of school. When I was able to return I was told not to run or engage in any type of strenuous activity. So, over the next few years I never learned to roller skate, or ride a bike, or participate in many activities that other children enjoyed. I remember standing by the fence surrounding the school yard and watching the girls play jump rope. Double Dutch was very popular, but I was destined to be a spectator while they showed off their jumping skills.

At home, I once again turned to reading books. Luckily, I got so much enjoyment from this, that it didn't matter that I missed out on some other things. I was perfectly content with my life. During the evening hours, the radio, which featured a different ongoing series every day of the week, was anticipated with much pleasure. At that time, years before the onset of television, the console radio was considered a marvel of technology.

Some of the shows which I remember with much nostalgia are Sherlock Holmes, the Lux Radio Theatre, Fibber McGee and Molly, The Shadow, The Green Hornet, Little Orphan Annie, and of course, one of the greatest classics of that era, The Jack Benny Show. In 1936 the BBC broadcast its first story. It concerned a fire at the Crystal Palace in London. The report included on-the-spot commentary, a prelude to today's evening news on all our major TV channels. In 1938 there were 650 transmitters and 26 million receivers in the United States. The radio served as a focal point for our day-to-day family gatherings, just as television serves that purpose today. I looked forward to sitting in front of the radio and enjoying the stories, or the news, or the music which was offered on a continual basis. This was my main contact to the outside world, and I partook of it as much as I possibly could.

Franklin D. Roosevelt, the only president to occupy the White House for four terms, was known for his Fireside Chats. He used this time to apprise his listeners of important policy decisions and important happenings here at home and abroad. This commentary was our lifeline to important worldwide happenings. I'm certain that no one still alive after so many years will ever forget FDR's voice telling the nation on December 7th, 1941, that the Japanese had bombed Pearl Harbor. With that announcement, our country entered the Second World War. We would never be the same again.

CHAPTER FOUR

❧❦

Indeed, our entrance into the war changed everyone's lives. Many young men rushed to their local Army recruiting center, and signed up to serve their country. My brother, Bernie, was among them. At eighteen he volunteered for the U.S. Air Force. After a brief training period he was shipped overseas, and found himself stationed in North Africa. Bernie served as a tail gunner. He wrote home regularly, but said little about the missions on which he flew. This was just as well, since each mission placed him in harm's way. Needless to say, my parents were very anxious during this period.

The war was being fought on several fronts. It was waged on land, on sea, and in the air. Over the next year many cities fell to the German and Japanese forces. Those of us living in the United States listened helplessly to the world news. Here at home many items were rationed. We were given ration books for butter, and cheese, and meat. Nylon stockings, tires, and many other items were in short supply. Women stepped in to fill the massive vacancies in the workplace, while men were fighting overseas. One of the songs that rose to popularity was "Rosie, the Riveter," a ballad honoring the many females working on the home front, producing the airplanes and other items that were needed to wage the worldwide conflict.

Shortly after the onset of World War II, our neighbor across the street signed up for service in the Navy. Ernie was a young man in his twenties. His parents owned the grocery store directly across from us, but for some reason we never became too friendly. I just knew Ernest and his parents on a fairly casual basis. During this era when someone in the household went into the service, this fact was recognized by hanging a small flag in the window. The flag contained a single blue star on a white background. If that person was killed in action, the blue star was replaced by a gold star. I'll never forget the day I walked past Ernie's house, and saw the gold star in the window. It's one thing to hear the casualties announced over the radio. Even though you know it's someone's son or brother, it's not the same when you can put a face to it. Ernie was one of thousands who paid the ultimate price for our final victory in 1945. Some sixty years after World War II, I still remember Ernie, and the sacrifice he made for all of us.

Women also served in the Armed Forces. The female component of the Army was known as WAC's (Women's Army Corps), and the navy had the WAVES. These women did not serve on the front lines. Instead, they served in an auxiliary capacity, and helped with food, uniforms, living quarters, pay and medical care.

During this turbulent time, my sister, Clara, had graduated from high school. Following her graduation, she entered nurse's training at Jewish Hospital in Philadelphia. Currently, this site is known as Albert Einstein Medical Center. With so many nurses needed during wartime, there was a tremendous shortage of nurses to care for the population at home.

In 1943 the Federal Government established the Cadet Nurse Corps within the Public Health Service. During the next five years, over 100,000 nurses graduated from the Corps, making it one of the most fruitful Federal nursing programs in history. The Cadet Nurse Corps granted scholarships and stipends to qualified applicants in exchange for providing essential civilian nursing services for the duration of the war. Clara availed herself of these benefits, and joined the Corps in order to complete her nurse's training. Like the WACs and the WAVES, the Cadet Nurses were given cool-looking uniforms, and I beamed with pride when I first saw Clara wearing her uniform.

Because of the acute nursing shortage, Clara worked many long hours at the hospital. If there was emergency surgery needed in the middle of the night,

Clara, who had already worked all day, would be asked to come to the Operating Room to assist. It was hard on all the nurses to carry this extra burden. Over a period of many months, her health suffered, and Clara eventually began to pass out at work. There was no clear cut diagnosis given, but it was obvious she needed to return home and get adequate rest. Thus, she was granted a leave of absence, and sent back home.

Although I was sorry that Clara was sick, it was great to have her back home again. The two of us were always able to have long discussions, and I was always able to tell her things I couldn't say to anyone else.

Clara, like myself, had very deep feelings about many things. She felt her mission in life was to become a nurse, and she was determined to fulfill this mission, no matter what obstacles stood in her way. She also had a premonition that she would die at a young age, and that God wanted her to become an extraordinary nurse during her lifetime. Clara was not only an extraordinary nurse, she was an extraordinary person. She was very loving and warm, and had an enormous amount of compassion for others.

When she first came home, I watched in horror several times, as she would stiffen and fall over, without any warning. This was one of several medical mysteries that befell Clara during her lifetime. It was very scary to watch. However, eventually this phenomenon passed, and she returned to good health. Having witnessed this harrowing experience, Mom did not want Clara to return to nursing. But Clara was determined to complete what she believed to be her destiny. And complete it, she did.

CHAPTER FIVE

I was ten years old when the United States entered the war. At that time I was in the fifth grade. By the time the war ended, I was a young teenager, a senior in the junior high school I attended. As I grew older I discovered that I had a flair for, and a love of writing. I was active on the school newspaper throughout junior and senior high school. As I mentioned before, since I was growing up in a neighborhood which was primarily occupied by people of color, I always had a problem befriending anyone who displayed racial prejudice. When I attended grade school, I had no white friends. I was constantly surrounded by boys and girls whose skins were various shades of tan and brown. I still find it very amusing that white folks spend long hours lying in the sun, or else pay money for the services of a tanning salon, in order to acquire a darker pigment to their skins, in an era where racial prejudice still exists. Apparently, it's nice to have a tan skin, except if you were born that way by the grace of God. Does that make any sense?

I was not only one of the few white children in my neighborhood, I was being raised Jewish amidst a sea of Christians. The boundary at that time in West Philadelphia was Market Street. The population north of Market Street, where we lived, was basically black, and south of Market Street, was predominately white with many Jewish sections. Since we lived close to Market Street, it was only a short walk to Beth Judah, the small neighborhood synagogue. My dad would take me to Saturday morning services, and once I turned ten I was enrolled in Hebrew School. I enjoyed learning Hebrew and being able to doven, or pray in Hebrew, and to sing the many songs which were part of the service, especially during the holidays. In those days, girls did not celebrate their Bat Mitzvah at age thirteen, as they do today, My only claim to fame was during Chanukah, when I was chosen to lead the congregation in the blessing which was sung during the lighting of the candles. This was a special honor for me and I thoroughly enjoyed it.

I've always loved to sing, and apparently my mom thought I was pretty good. I remember that when she was busy in the kitchen preparing dinner, I would often serenade her with one of the songs which were popular over the airwaves. During the war, when London was being bombed on a continual basis, there was a song titled "The White Cliffs of Dover," which was very poignant and beautiful. I sang the haunting lyrics many times, hoping and praying, along with the British people for the day when peace, along with the bluebirds, would return to the cliffs of Dover. Eventually, the warfare did end, and an Armistice was declared. There was joy from coast to coast when this day arrived. My family, along with millions of others, breathed a sigh of relief that their loved ones, who had served in the armed forces would soon be returning home. It was with sadness, though, that we remembered that two cities in Japan had been hit by an atomic bomb. Yes, it had ended the war, but this bombing had killed and maimed so many innocent civilians. A heavy price to pay, indeed.

While all of this was going on in the outside world, there was an ongoing struggle taking place deep inside of me. I can't really say when it started. Even as a very young child I wondered, if there is only one God, why did mankind have so many religions? Why did I go to a synagogue when so many of the children I knew attended various churches? Don't misunderstand. As I said before, I really enjoyed attending synagogue. However, I always felt that something was missing, that there was more—something more encompassing. I always had an inquisitive mind. While Jewish people generally don't go outside of their own religion, I didn't recognize any boundaries.

As always, my zest for reading continued. I read a good bit about Catholicism and accepted everything I read. It didn't seem at all strange to me that I would go to Temple in the morning, and spend the afternoon boning up on Christianity, and the

Catholic religion, in particular. As a matter of fact, I can recall spending much time thinking in depth of becoming a nun. I fantasized about wearing the habit of a nun, and spending my life married to the church. After all, Jesus was born Jewish, and lived his life as a Jew. Somehow my nature has always been spiritual, and becoming a nun seemed like the right thing to do. By taking this one huge step, I would continue to function on a spiritual plane through the rest of my life. Deep down, I really wanted to do this.

There was only one small problem. I couldn't tell anyone, especially my parents. I think my mother would have had a heart attack. It was assumed I would marry a nice Jewish boy, and raise children in the Jewish tradition. So it was; I was not able to speak of this to anyone. However, my concept of one God, and one house of worship for all, which was formed early in my childhood, would remain with me for many years to come. It was not just a childish notion. It was part and parcel of who I was to become.

CHAPTER SIX

My years in Junior High school, today called Middle School, were uneventful. I discovered my love of writing, and enjoyed working on the school newspaper. Finally, I had to decide on a curriculum. Many girls chose the commercial curriculum, which involved taking typing, shorthand, and bookkeeping. My preference was to go with the academic route, with the hope that I would go to college when I graduated from high school. I knew that it would be an uphill battle to convince my mom that this was an appropriate goal for me.

Mom, like so many women in the forties, thought that women should get married and raise a family, leaving men to get an education, have a career, and be the breadwinner. Only a small number of women worked outside of the home, once married. I breathed a sigh of relief when my mother said I could study the academic subjects, providing I also added typing to my curriculum. That choice actually served me well in the years that followed.

Once I completed my junior high years I entered Overbrook High School. Since the junior high I attended was located south of Market Street, mostly all of my classmates were assigned to attend West Philadelphia High School. As I lived north of Market Street, I was assigned to attend Overbrook High. It was a distance from my house, but easily reached by the "G" bus which was only a block away.

It was a lonely feeling going into a new school not knowing anyone. Many of the youngsters attending Overbrook lived in Wynnefield. While many of the homes there were row homes, there were also single homes. The area was considered to be upscale as many professional, well-to-do people made their home in that section.

I was extremely shy to begin with. So trying to mix it up with the "in" crowd, many of whom had known each other since childhood, was difficult. To make matters worse, I felt very self-conscious about my house. To say the house and furnishings were modest, would be a considerable understatement. So, when most of the kids didn't bother with me, in a way, it was a relief. Thankfully, there was none of the meanness which seems prevalent in today's schools.

Before too long I met Jane, with whom I became fast friends. She was tall, with long blond hair, and ever so sweet. She was also shy by nature, but together we were chatter boxes, sharing with each other all of our hopes and dreams for the unknown years that lay ahead.

When I was sixteen I began dating. I met Joe when I was in the eleventh grade. He was a year ahead of me but we attended one class together. Joe was extremely handsome. He had black hair and beautiful blue eyes. His features were striking. Above all, he was a smooth talker.

We enjoyed all of the things teenage couples did. We went out for pizza, and to the movies, and school events, mostly basketball games. Overbrook at that time had outstanding basketball players, some of whom went on to play professionally. Wilt Chamberlain was just a few years behind me.

When Joe graduated from school, he got a job as an outside salesman for a large novelty company in downtown Philadelphia. We started going to more expensive places like the Latin Casino, which featured many superstars of that era, like Harry Belafonte. It was very exciting to see him in person. Having been so sheltered growing up, being able to partake of the night life in Philly was a welcome addition to my world. I had one or two drinks during the night, but never had the desire to drink more. I guess I was lucky. My parents never smoked or drank anything but wine, and usually that was on holidays. Somehow, I was comfortable following their example.

As time went on, I noticed that Joe had an active imagination. Among other things, he told me that his family traveled with the circus for years. Like so many of the things he told me, it turned out to be a complete fabrication. As time went on, I realized I couldn't believe anything he told me. However, he was a charmer, and Mom and Dad thought he was great. I dated a few other young men in the beginning, during the time I dated Joe, but didn't feel overly impressed with any of them.

At this time, I was completing my senior year in high school. We were encouraged to apply to the college, or colleges, of our choice. However, as I suspected, Mom would have none of it. Years earlier, when Eleanor wanted to go to college and become a teacher, Mom vehemently opposed the idea. Ellie was brilliant and caring. She would have made an excellent teacher. However, once out of school, she went on to become a bookkeeper. She worked for a nearby firm for a while, and then took the giant step of leaving home and moving to Brooklyn. At that time, I was left to fend for myself.

I loved the sciences. In my heart, I knew I wanted to be a doctor. However, I knew my mother would never support my dream. So, I looked into becoming a lab technician, which would have required a minimal amount of training. That, also, did not fly. It was useless to try to change her mind.

I remember sitting in Spanish class with Mr. Contini. He inquired how many of us would be attending college. When I didn't raise my hand, he was noticeably surprised. Obviously, thinking that finances were the primary reason, he offered me a scholarship for Spanish, on the spot. It had been one of my favorite subjects, and I had always done well. I was excited at the idea of getting a scholarship, but Mom had decided that women going to college was a waste of time.

She had spent her whole life being a housewife—cooking and cleaning, and raising her children. She had no other ambitions. She lived in her own little world, and couldn't understand why anybody would want more. So, regretfully, I turned down the prospect of a scholarship. I was much too weak to defy my mother's wishes. It was much easier to do what she wanted, as I had done so many times before.

Clara, like Eleanor, was no longer at home. She had completed her nurse's training and was now working in her chosen profession. She had had the backbone to stand up to my mother, and carve out the career to which she felt she had been called.

CHAPTER SEVEN

❧❧

A s I reached the completion of my senior year I continued to date Joe. On a superficial level, we enjoyed being with each other. But as the months progressed, it became clear that we lived by different value standards. I was intrinsically honest, while Joe saw nothing wrong with getting what he wanted by lying and cheating.

For some reason which I will never understand, he decided he wanted to marry me. We were not intimate, and I certainly was not in love with him. I was painfully shy, and I certainly didn't have many men interested in me. So Joe had become a companion and a friend. And I wanted nothing more. When he surprised me with a proposal, my answer was an emphatic "No!" I told him I did not want to continue seeing him, and I assumed that was the end of our involvement with each other.

Naturally, I gave this information to my parents, and asked that they not let him enter the house should he come back again. And come back, he did indeed! And, in case you haven't guessed it, my mom had no problem letting him come upstairs to the living room we had created on the second floor.

Yes indeed! Mom had found a man eager to marry her daughter, and she was delighted at the prospect. I explained to her that I did not love him, and that his constant lying was something I didn't want to live with. For years, my mother had always put me down. No matter what I did, it was never good enough for her. But her next remark cut me like a knife.

"Rose, if you don't marry him, you might not find anyone else who will want to. You don't want to be an old maid, do you?"

Being raised in that house had already demolished any self-esteem I might have been able to achieve. But for once in my life I tried to stand up to my mother. I felt I deserved better than a liar and a cheater as my husband. But with Mom's encouragement, Joe kept coming back to the house. He persisted in his quest to become engaged, and eventually I caved in, just as I had done so many times before. It takes a powerful person to stand up to my mother, and through years of brain-washing I had become very submissive. It was the only way I knew to cope!

Thus, unhappily, I became engaged, and shortly thereafter, set a date for my marriage. Upon graduating high school, I got a job working on the counter for Metropolitan Life Insurance. I took care of customers who paid for their insurance one month at a time. I met a lot of people this way, and being a "people person" I totally enjoyed it. The years I had spent working in the store with my dad had paid off.

The weeks rolled on, and I became busy making plans for my wedding. Dad and I booked an available site. The ceremony and reception would be at the caterer's home base in Wynnefield. I allowed myself to be swept up in the excitement of buying a wedding gown and making all of the necessary arrangements. But, deep down inside, I knew it was a mistake. I felt like a lamb being led to the slaughter.

A few months before the wedding I got a sudden, unexpected phone call. The person on the other end identified himself as a teacher named "Jim." It turns out Jim had been on the bus with me every morning as I made my trek to Overbrook High for my studies. Apparently shy, he had never spoken to me, but had wanted to get to know me and date me. He was eventually able to get my name and phone number, and had gone out on a limb to call me.

Once I got over the surprise of the sudden contact, I explained that I was now engaged to be married. However, we did continue to talk, and eventually I did share with him my strong concern for the upcoming union. Jim encouraged me to follow my heart, and bring the wedding plans to a halt.

When I got up enough nerve, I told Mom about the phone call. I started sobbing and told her once again I didn't want to marry Joe. As if she didn't know that!! But her answer was, "You can't break off your engagement. That would be a 'shonda.'"

'Shonda' is a Jewish word for disgrace. She was stunned I would suggest such a thing. Yes, back in the 1940s this was almost unheard of. Mother could have been the poster child for the multitude of people who care only about appearances. What would her family and friends think! After all, that was more important than caring about the happiness of your child. So, in the end she proceeded to sentence me to continue the sham, and exchange vows with someone who had dubious values. It is bad enough to get married when you are not aware of someone's faults. But in my case I can't say that. I knew exactly what I was getting into.

On September eleventh, 1949, I became Joe's wife. That date marked the beginning of the biggest mistake of my life. Little could I know that more than fifty years later, the date, September 11th, would mark the worst terrorist attack to take place on American soil. What a weird coincidence!

CHAPTER EIGHT

For better or worse, the wedding took place. And with it I vowed to do my best to make it work. I continued to work for a short time until I found that I was pregnant. I gave birth to a healthy baby boy, whom we named Stephen. Joe had very little interaction with his son, but I was very happy having a baby to care for. Like many women who find themselves in an unhappy marriage, having a child was looked at as a positive event. I was able to stay home and give my undivided attention to raising my first born son. I was determined to give him all the love that I felt a child needed to be nurtured properly. After Steve's birth we were able to purchase a lovely ranch home in the suburbs. We had adopted a collie, and the home had a large piece of ground on which Steve and his dog could play to their heart's content.

Several years passed, and without warning, I learned that Joe had lost his job. He didn't seem terribly concerned, and announced that he would open his own business! He found a partner who was willing to put up money. Together, they started a wholesale toy business. He never disclosed any of the details, like where did he get his share of the money? It was obvious my con artist husband had managed to get his hands on money that was not earned on the straight and narrow path. I had no idea what he did, but getting fired was a pretty good clue. There was no use asking. I was kept in the dark, and perhaps it was just as well, since I would not have supported his shady dealings.

Joe was out on business a lot of the time. Although I enjoyed being with my toddler full time, I missed having adult companionship. Mom suggested we move back to the city, as it would be easier for her to visit. She never learned to drive, and could only get around by public transportation. Eventually, I decided that moving back to the city would have its advantages. I did not have a car, and felt isolated from the area around me. With that decision made, Joe and I bought a property in Overbrook Park. Shopping was within walking distance and the bus stopped right at my front door. I was able to do many things that I was unable to do before. Life for me became much more palatable.

It was a very nice house, in a good neighborhood, and we were able to make lots of friends. Since I am a people person, this is essential for my well-being. Also, the stores were within walking distance, and it was a pleasure to be able to stroll along the main avenue in nice weather and peek into the store windows.

In the meantime, my sister, Clara, who had married some years earlier, had moved to Bridgeport, Connecticut, with her husband, Bernard, and her son, Mark. Bernie was an electrical engineer, and Clara continued to do private duty nursing, plus she volunteered her time at the Red Cross Blood Bank in Bridgeport.

Some years earlier, Clara had developed a bleeding problem of unknown origin. She was seen by the best doctors available at the time, but despite numerous tests, they were unable to ascertain the cause of her rectal bleeding. Since it was, apparently, a gastrological problem, she eventually underwent exploratory surgery, so doctors could open her up and examine all of her organs. This was years before MRIs came into being; and in order to get a diagnosis, this type of surgery was fairly commonplace. However, the surgery yielded no clues as to her abnormal bleeding. She was told there was no sign of any abnormality, and that she shouldn't be too concerned about it.

In the summer of 1954 I went up to Bridgeport to visit her. Clara was very special in my life, and I missed having her close by. On the second day of my visit we went for a walk in the park. At one point, we stopped to rest. I was sitting across from her. As we sat there chatting, I was astonished by what I saw. There was blood oozing out of the sweat glands on her leg! Alarmed I said, "Clara, there is blood coming out of your leg."

She looked down, took out a tissue, and wiped it away. I was waiting for an explanation, but she simply said, "This has been happening lately. I don't know why."

I was shocked by what I had seen. I had never seen anything like it. What could it mean? Clara, who had been experiencing unusual bleeding episodes for half a dozen years, had learned to accept this strange phenomenon as part of her life. There was no known answer. So, my visit continued, and I went home happy that we had gotten to spend some time together. However, I was very puzzled and worried by what I had witnessed.

As I mentioned earlier, Joe and I had a nice circle of friends with whom we would get together on a fairly regular basis. Several months after my visit to Bridgeport, we entertained two of these couples in our home. We had some refreshments and some drinks, and were sitting in the living room having a pleasant conversation. What happened next has been etched into my memory forever.

I clearly remember sitting on the piano bench, facing our guests. Suddenly, while we were quietly talking, the room was filled with the sound of a bird chirping. The sound was all around us in the room, but there was nothing to be seen which could be the cause. One of our companions asked, "Do you have a tea kettle on?" I shook my head in a negative response. I felt completely mystified. There was no bird in the house. Nor was there anything else which could have been responsible for the sound.

I looked at my watch and saw it was nine o'clock. The chirping had lasted for a minute or so, and then stopped. We went back to our conversation, enjoying each other's company. Our company left around eleven-thirty, and I was doing a few dishes, and straightening up our home. It was a few minutes before midnight when our phone rang. When I answered I found Bernie, Clara's husband, on the other end. He told me that Clara was in the hospital.

Earlier in the evening, as she was bathing Mark, she grabbed her head and said she had a horrible headache. She asked Mark to get his daddy. Bernie rushed upstairs and found his wife unconscious on the floor.

She was rushed to the hospital by ambulance. After being seen by the doctors in the ER, Bernie was advised that Clara had suffered a major cerebral hemorrhage, apparently caused by an aneurism, and that there was nothing that could be done. She would pass away shortly, and was apparently already brain dead.

I told Bernie that I would check to see when I could get a train to Bridgeport, but found there would not be any service until morning. Before I hung up, I asked him what time she had collapsed in the bathroom. The answer came back, "It was nine o'clock." Could it be that although Clara's body was being kept alive in the hospital, her soul had departed hours earlier, and on her way to her eternal rest, she had stopped for a moment to bid farewell to her little sister? There was no earthly explanation for what had been witnessed by a room full of people. But the event shows that there is more to life and death than we can know in this world. Some people believe that when we take our last breath here on earth, that is the end. But clearly this is not so. Although our time here on earth has passed, our life in the spiritual realm has just begun.

That evening totally transformed my life. Clara had always known she would die early in life, but no one believed her, especially me. I was twenty-two and Clara was twenty-nine when her prediction became reality. She was a very spiritual person, who truly believed that she was sent here by God to be a nurse, and minister to those who were sick and needy. She told Bernie a week prior to her death that she was an angel sent by the Lord, and that she had fulfilled her mission here on earth. I believe that part of her mission was to serve as my teacher. The things which she shared with me had a very profound effect on my life. She did not want anyone to cry for her, but, of course we did. It is now over fifty years since that fateful day, but I remember it like it was yesterday. It was definitely a life altering experience. Clara's life had touched so many people with her loving and caring ways. She set an example for others. Her passing made me realize that it is not important how long we live, but rather what we do with the years we are given. Her life was an inspiration to me to live life to the fullest, and to give as much as possible to others. This is what makes your life worthwhile. This is what lives on when you are gone.

CHAPTER NINE

Clara passed away on October 11, 1954. By some miracle Joe and I had been married for five years and Steve was now three years old. Raising him was a very worthwhile challenge. I was determined to give him what I had never had—self-confidence. Although I had been married at eighteen and became a mother at twenty, I was doing just fine. What's more, I was developing confidence in myself. I made a mental list of what qualities were important for people to have; for instance, intelligence, humor, compassion, a willingness to help others, being honest and trustworthy, etc. When I measured myself against that list, I realized I scored very well. It made me realize I probably undervalued myself. I felt I was I good wife and mother, and my interest in others made it easy for me to make friends. I must be doing something right.

Because of my childhood insecurity, I developed a keen interest in the whole area of self-esteem. I wondered how many other people had grown up with a feeling of inferiority. During my years in Overbrook Park, I did my own little survey. Whenever I had the opportunity to have a meaningful conversation with someone, I managed to steer the conversation to feelings of inferiority. What I found amazed me. So many men and women who gave the outward appearance of confidence did not possess that confidence inwardly. It seemed apparent that poor self-esteem was extremely widespread.

Years later, in studying psychology, I found that Alfred Adler spent much of his life in the study and importance of this negative attribute. Adler, himself, was weak and frequently ill as a toddler, and struggled with feelings of inferiority when comparing himself to his older brother, who was much stronger. This led to his theory that young children often feel inferior to those around them. It appeared that my findings were backed up by a very prominent psychiatrist of his time.

Adler believed that there are two ways to overcome these feelings. One way is to strive for success by working for the betterment of mankind. The second way is to strive for superiority. The latter approach is not considered healthy since it only focuses on personal achievement.

Our society is full of people who are trying to be superior to others. They need to buy the latest car, the biggest house, the most expensive jewelry, etc. But, in comparing themselves to others, there is someone with a better car, a bigger house, and more expensive clothes and jewelry. So, they can never be satisfied. Also, those who need to feel better about themselves use criticism of others to boost their own feelings of inadequacy. The end result is racism, sexism, and ageism. How wonderful it makes them feel to put down other groups of people. Reminds you of Hitler, doesn't it? He needed a master race to prove how great he was. Millions died because of his need for a master race. And what we learned was that he was, indeed, very sick.

Once you have achieved good self-esteem, you do not have a need to put others down. You arrive at a plateau where you realize that all men and women, although very diverse, are all equal. You realize it is foolish to compare yourself to others. God has created everyone with various strengths, as well as various weaknesses. It is virtually impossible to compare people. Some are extremely intelligent, others shine in athletics. Still others are very creative; many may be artistic. Just because you can't paint like Rembrandt, doesn't make you an inferior person. Maybe you make the best cookies for the PTA. The list goes on and on. You may drive a truck, carrying food that we all need, program a computer, be a top-notch salesman (which definitely helps our economy) etc. All of our work is important. Most of all, you may be a great mom or dad. We've already discussed how important that is. It is one of the most important jobs in the world. If we use our God-given talent to the best of our ability, we will have lived a life that is worthwhile.

If possible, we should give back to society. Yes, one way to help others is to donate money. But money alone, is not enough. Perhaps even more important is your time. Each of us can make a contribution to others. There are endless ways in which volunteers can be used. One can work in a food bank, read to young children, tutor other young ones who can use a little extra help, visit the elderly in a nursing home, or work in a phone bank for a good cause. Find a way in which you can create a service for your favorite charity. It is a great feeling.

Unfortunately, there are many people in the world who are misfits. They are only interested in themselves and their own well-being. It doesn't matter who they hurt in following their own agenda. My husband, Joseph, was one of them. As time went on, Joe was spending less and less time at home. He claimed he was working late, but somewhere inside, I knew it was one of his lies.

One evening he told me he was planning to attend a wholesale toy show at a local hotel. That night I had to ask him about something, so I placed a phone call to the hotel. With a great deal of disappointment I learned there was no such show at the hotel. Joe was busted!

Although I believe in the sanctity of marriage, surely being faithful to each other is one of the main components of such a union. My initial fears were realized; Joe's dubious character had come to fruition.

By the end of our seventh year, I had had enough. I filed for divorce.

I would have to find a job to support Steve and myself. But I hoped Joe would be man enough to help with the support of his son. There were mortgage payments to be made, utilities to pay, and food and clothing to buy. However, by the time we appeared before a judge, Joe had managed to siphon off money from his business (unknown to his partner). With a straight face he told the judge the once thriving business was on the verge of bankruptcy.

Since there was no proof to the contrary, Joe was ordered to pay twenty dollars per week for Steve's support. It was a sham, but very much in keeping with Joe's egocentric character. He was pleased that he managed to pull one over on me. Even though the payment the judge ordered wasn't nearly enough to support our child, I was glad my life with Joe was over. It was very disheartening to live with a liar and a cheat, and I was happy that this chapter of my life was now behind me.

CHAPTER TEN

❧

Following my divorce I was able to get a good job in Center City Philadelphia. I was hired by a well-known printing company where I was to function as an administrative assistant to the president and owner. The job was interesting, and my boss was very nice. It was a good lifestyle, and I felt very content. Mom cared for Steve until I returned home from work, but Joe did not visit Steve or keep in touch with him. My heart ached for him. Although Joe was not a good father, he was the only father Steve would ever have. I was still in my mid-twenties. Maybe someday I would find a man who would accept Steve, and love him as his own son. Every child deserves that.

Eventually, I started dating. I attended dances for singles given by one of the synagogues. I loved to dance. So, not only was it great fun, it was certainly an easy way to meet eligible men. However, I felt very self-conscious about the fact that I had a son. I felt that most men would not want the responsibility of raising a child that was not theirs. But it did not seem to be a deterrent to most of the men I met. Eventually, I met the man who would become my future husband. His name was Sandy, and we had that spark that told us we were right for each other. We started dating, but having been burned once, I was somewhat hesitant at the prospects of a happy marriage. However, Sandy was really great with Steve. If he would be asked a question, he would very patiently answer him. This was definitely very reassuring. Sandy and I dated for about a year before he popped the question. I did not hesitate to give him a positive answer.

Indeed, Sandy had bonded with Steve, and the two of them got along quite well. Things had worked out, after all. I felt very blessed. On April 5, 1959, Sandy and I got married in front of family and friends, and started our life together.

We decided to keep the house in Overbrook Park, because it was a lovely house, and Steve was attending the elementary school right across the street. Talk about convenience! It had been a struggle to maintain the house after my divorce, but somehow I managed to do it.

Sandy was a college graduate, with a degree in journalism. He was working as a reporter for a small out-of-town newspaper. We took a brief honeymoon, and returned home to begin married life. It was less than a month later that Sandy found himself without a job. He was working in a difficult field. There was no guarantee of a long and stable career as a reporter. We talked about this for a long time. Sandy decided to return to school to get a Master's degree in teaching. Although teaching didn't pay very well, at least once hired, the job would be permanent. Since he already had a Bachelor's degree, he would be able to do substitute teaching until he earned the required credits. Once again, life had thrown me a curve ball, but there was a solution.

Sandy started teaching, and life was uneventful. I had taken a job with an ad agency, and all was going well. I wanted to have a sibling for Steve. But that didn't happen right away. I continued to work outside the home until I finally became pregnant. I worked up until my last month, and then quit my job. My desire was to be a full time mom once again. My second child, a healthy baby boy, came into the world on October 11, 1961. We named him Michael. It was very unnerving to have him born on October 11th. I was very much aware that this was the same date on which Clara had passed away. It was a weird feeling. But Michael was healthy, and that was all that really mattered. God had called home someone I loved, but now I was given a precious bundle, who would grow to be a joy in my life. The date was one of many coincidences.

The birth of another son was, indeed, a happy event. Michael was a happy child and very easy to care for. However, like most young couples, we thought it would be nice to add a little girl to the mix. Since I had already passed my thirtieth birthday, I didn't want to wait too long. Therefore, finding out there was another baby on the way was a happy discovery. The newest addition to the family was due to arrive in mid-February, 1963. At last I would have the family of my dreams. Motherhood suited me completely. Sandy was now working steadily, and our boys were thriving. I was on top of the world!

By the time I was in my fourth month I had quite a large baby bump. My obstetrician, Dr. Mitchell, acknowledged the baby appeared to be large. This was years before ultrasounds were available. What was happening inside remained a mystery to both doctor and mother-to-be. The months rolled on, and Dr. Mitchell would check me out thoroughly during each visit. He would listen intently to my abdomen with his stethoscope. If there were twins, the heart rate of one might be different from the second. But, there was nothing audible to be learned. So, at the beginning of month eight, he ordered an x-ray. X-rays were not safe to be done on an expectant mother before that.

Twenty-four hours later I heard the news I had anticipated. I was carrying twins. One was lying with his head pointing downward, in the normal birth position. The second fetus was in a breach position. He or she was upright in my womb. I told Sandy the news. He thought I was joking. Finally, I convinced him I wasn't kidding. He didn't know what to say.

The doctor now saw me every week. I was not a very big woman. I stood at 5'2" and only weighed about one hundred pounds at the start of my pregnancy. Due to my petite size, Dr. Mitchell said I would probably not be able to carry the babies to full term. Once I learned I was carrying twins, I began to be very concerned. Both Steve and Mike weighed a little over six pounds at birth. The twins would probably be born a month or more prematurely. That was really scary! How much would they weigh? During the sixties, babies of low birth weight did not survive. Jacqueline Kennedy had a baby while she and her husband, John F. Kennedy, occupied the White House. This baby was born prematurely and died.

I said a fervent prayer every day for the well-being of my unborn children. The good Lord answered my prayer. David and Larry entered the world on January 12, 1963. David tipped the scales at five and a half pounds. Larry was a few ounces lighter than his brother. That I was able to carry two babies of this size was nothing short of a miracle. There are no words to describe the happiness I felt. God gave them the gift of life, and, in return, during their adult life they have sung His praises, and served Him. But I am getting ahead of myself.

CHAPTER ELEVEN

As with most newborns, the twins lost a little weight during their first few days in the nursery.

When it was time for me to leave the hospital, David, who was two minutes older than Larry and slightly heavier, was found to be thriving well, and he was allowed to go home with me. However, the pediatrician decided it would be best if Larry could remain a few days longer.

Michael was happy to have his mommy home again, and he even accepted this little intruder in his life who would have to be picked up and changed and fed by his mother, while he waited patiently to have her all to himself again. I tried to shower Michael with a lot of attention so that he wouldn't feel jealous of his baby brother. All was going well until the time came to get Larry, and bring him home.

Finally, the big day arrived. I felt overjoyed that our youngest child was finally joining the rest of the family. Sandy and I made one last trip to the hospital, where we dressed Larry and carried him to the car for the short trip to our house. The doctor had told me not to go up and down the steps for another few days. Therefore, it made sense to keep the twins downstairs for the time being. We set up a second carriage about a foot away from the first, and put Larry, now sound asleep, into it.

Shortly after our arrival, Michael came into the room. He peeked into the carriage where David was sleeping. Then he went over to the second carriage where Larry was also asleep. Michael then looked at me with a look that I will never forget. His eyes were wide with wonder. He was a fifteen month old toddler. He was simply too young to understand that his mommy, whose tummy had grown larger and larger over the past eight months, had given birth to not one, but two babies, and that as time progressed he would be the big brother to these little bundles, who were now dozing peacefully in their carriages.

Who knows what he was thinking as he watched this unexpected phenomenon. Perhaps, "Every time Mommy goes away, she comes back with another baby. Where are they coming from? There must be a baby garden somewhere where you go and pick up as many babies as you want. I wonder if she will go out tomorrow and come home with another baby."

Even though four decades have passed since that January day, I can still see that expression of amazement on Mike's face. And the story of his first look at his twin brothers side by side, has been told and retold many times.

Life with two babies and a toddler was very busy, indeed. Disposable diapers were not yet in use. Babies wore cloth diapers at this time in history. There were diaper services available, who would wash the diapers and return them the following week. But with three children in diapers, the number of diapers required for a week was huge, and the cost was exorbitant. Hence, on a teacher's salary, this service was beyond our means.

So every morning began with a load of diapers being soaked and washed and dried. By the time the twins had come along, which was twelve years after Stephen's birth, we were fortunate enough to own a dryer. Earlier, diapers had to be hung out on the line to dry. This is what was necessary when Steve was a baby. During the winter, the diapers used to come in feeling like pieces of cardboard, which had to be warmed and folded. Thank goodness for the dryer when it arrived.

Anybody who has cared for one baby knows there is a lot of work involved. Imagine having two, plus a toddler, plus a twelve year old, and a husband to boot who was determined to follow in his father's footsteps. My father-in-law believed that caring for children was woman's work. Growing up in this environment, Sandy managed to instill this macho theory into his brain. So, even though I was worn out to the point of exhaustion, Sandy would inform me that he had to rest when he came home, because he had to work the next day. What did he think I was doing? I never really knew, but the role of caretaker, cook, housekeeper, and laundress became my exclusive territory.

Still, here I am writing about it, so obviously I survived. At least Sandy didn't cheat on me, so I am grateful for that. And in spite of all the work, the children were a joy. Some memories of those early days stand out above all others. I remember a number of times while I was holding one of the twins, Michael would appear and ask for something. I got the feeling that he was testing me. Who was more important? I had no problem with that. I would put down the baby and get whatever Mike wanted. After a while he stopped doing this. Apparently, he had gotten his answer. He knew that his mommy still cared about him. I made sure he knew that he could never be replaced in my heart.

Time marched on and soon Larry and David were walking and running. The three boys formed a strong bond with each other. Many times I was asked if they were triplets. The house was like a mini-nursery and was very lively with the goings on of the children. The one person who resented all of this activity was Stephen. He had happily been an only child for ten years, and now so much of my attention was focused on his brothers. He spent a lot of time with his friends. The age difference was large, and he had nothing in common with his younger brothers. It wasn't hard to sense that he resented these interlopers into his life. But again, instead of offering to help out, he drew upon Sandy as a role model, and left all of the work to his mother. Was it any surprise that when Steve eventually married, he brought along all of this negative baggage which he acquired growing up? Unfortunately, our childhood often determines what we do in later life. However, we can learn to turn it around. One of the lessons I have learned is that we can determine our own fate. This is what I was able to do. Although my childhood made me feel insecure and inferior, I now see myself as equal to any man or woman. I have been able to grow and become the person I was meant to be.

CHAPTER TWELVE

Steve was twelve when Larry and David were born. So, a little over a year later he stood on the "bema" (altar) and celebrated his Bar Mitzvah. It was a very joyful occasion, and friends and family gathered later at a function to honor the Bar Mitzvah boy.

The synagogue where this occasion occurred was on the same block where we lived. When the twins passed their fourth birthday they were enrolled in the nursery school which operated on this site. Since Larry and David spent every waking moment together I asked that they be placed in different rooms during school hours so they could learn to function independently of each other.

To my surprise, when I returned to pick them up, I found them in the same room. Apparently, each of them had cried so hard, the teachers couldn't bear to keep them apart. They remained together for the remainder of the school year.

One afternoon, when I returned to take them home, I learned that David had gotten into trouble. Earlier in the day, one of Larry's playmates had picked up a toy telephone and hit him with it. David, upon learning of the incident, went to the child who had done this nasty thing to his brother; whereupon he lifted up the phone and hit the child with it. David had always been a very quiet, well behaved child. That he saw fit to do this to avenge the wrong done to his sibling came as a surprise to me. However, this signified the very close bond the brothers had with each other; although this certainly didn't justify his action.

Time passed, and the three boys moved on to elementary school. There was only one kindergarten in the school, so the twins stayed together for yet another year. However, when they entered first grade, they were placed in different classrooms. As I walked them across the street at the start of their school day, each one cried uncontrollably at the thought of having to separate from each other. This went on every day for at least a week. Passersby would look at me, wondering what was happening to precipitate such an outcry. I was thankful when the crying came to a halt.

Once they got used to being in separate classrooms they adjusted very well to school and did very well academically. Each one wanted to get the best grades possible, so they studied and did their homework without any problems. They were very well rounded, and also enjoyed participating in sports. They joined a Little League and played baseball, along with their brother, Mike.

While the boys were growing and turning into young men, I was also growing. As stated earlier, it is apparent to me that God has created human beings with a variety of strengths and weaknesses. As I grew into maturity, I came to realize that one of the gifts I was given was in the realm of spirituality. I had learned a lot about what life is all about, and I had decided that, at some future date, I would like to write a book to answer that time-honored question, "What is the purpose of life?" Over the years, I had developed some very deep insights on this subject and I had a strong desire to share these reflections with others. I thought about using the title *The Answer*.

One day I revealed this goal to my mother. We were having lunch together in my home. As we chatted, my mom disclosed the following incident which had taken place some thirty-eight years earlier. Mom said she vividly recalled having a dream in which she saw several of her dead relatives. One of these relatives, which had passed on, said to her, "Anna, I am going to give you the answer." My mother never understood what this meant.

Two weeks after this dream, my mother found she was pregnant with me. I was blown away by this revelation. She had never told me about it because it did not mean anything to her. But it was right on target with the discussion we were having.

CHAPTER THIRTEEN

❧✦❧

Although our house in Overbrook Park was spacious and well constructed, there was one major problem with living there. It was a row house, with a concrete driveway in back, and no ground for the boys to run and play. Sandy was teaching in the Philadelphia school system, and did not want to move out of state. However, once he was transferred to a high school in Northeast Philadelphia, it was quite easy to cross the bridge from New Jersey to arrive at school in a timely manner.

So, after a brief period of house hunting we purchased a four bedroom single home in Cinnaminson, New Jersey. It was situated on a half acre lot, and afforded lots of room for the boys to play to their heart's content. All of us made the transition easily. The three younger siblings did well in school and made friends easily with the neighborhood children. Steve had graduated from high school in Philadelphia and was attending Philadelphia Community College. While there he established a relationship with another student. Her name was Diane, and she seemed to blend in easily with our family. During our first year in Cinnaminson the two of them got engaged, much to the delight of everyone.

Once Steve graduated from the community college, he applied for and got a job as a statistician with a major insurance company. Diane and Steve were now ready to plan their future. They purchased a house and were married the following year.

Life for the rest of us was very positive. I got a part time job in a lighting fixture showroom. I had a flair for decorating which I was able to put to use there. And I was still able to be home when the boys returned from school. It was an ideal situation, and I was very content.

However, the question of religious diversity, which started in my childhood, still burned in my soul. If there was one God for mankind, then why did so many different religions exist? And why was this the cause of so much animosity? I visited churches of several denominations, and attended services at each one. I found it was a beautiful experience. Each service was uplifting, and spoke to me on a spiritual level. Never mind that I had been born to Jewish parents. My heart and soul yearned for the unity of all God's children: Christian, Jewish, Hindu, and Muslim.

As though in answer to this eternal question, I beheld a large billboard along a major highway. It spoke of the Baha'i Faith, and I was intrigued. What was this faith all about? Why had I never heard of it? I jotted down the phone number, and within the next few days I made a phone call to that number, a call which would change my life forever. The person who answered my inquiry referred me to someone who lived in a town directly adjacent to Cinnaminson.

At this number, I first established contact with Stephanie Gusky, a charming woman who was my age. She invited me to her home, where I was given several books and other written material outlining the major aspects of the Baha'i Faith. I knew that my search had led me to this time and place.

The Faith explained what has happened over the years from the time of Adam on. It is called Progressive Revelation. The Jewish people were the first to recognize the existence of one God, Yahweh. The Bible tells us that Abraham was the first of God's prophets on earth. He is considered the founding patriarch of the Israelites. When God appears he promises, "I will make of thee a great nation."

God has also appeared to other prophets. These prophets were Moses, who was also an Israelite, and Krishna who was prominent in the establishment of the Hindu religion. Zoroastrianism is based on the teachings of the prophet, Zoroaster. It was founded in the early part of the eighth century B.C. It served, in some form, as the national religion of the Iranian people, before it was gradually marginalized by Islam from the seventh century onwards.

Siddhatto Gautama is the spiritual teacher from Ancient India who founded Buddhism. In most Buddhist traditions, he is regarded as the Supreme Buddha. Buddha means "awakened one" or "enlightened one." He lived from 563 BC to 483 BC. He was followed by Jesus of Nazareth who lived from 5 BC to 30 AD. He is known worldwide as Jesus Christ. He is the central figure in Christianity. He is viewed as the Messiah which was foretold in the Old Testament.

Mohammed (570 - 632) is regarded by Muslims as a messenger and prophet of God. He is the founder of the religion of Islam. Muslims consider him the restorer of the uncorrupted monotheistic faith of Abraham, Moses, Jesus, and other prophets.

Baha'is talk about twin manifestations—the Bab (or Gate) who proclaimed His station in 1844 and Baha'u'llah who revealed His station as The Promised One in 1863. In short, Baha'is accept all of the Manifestations of God as being the messenger that was revealed to the world at a particular time in our existence. Baha'u'llah is God's messenger for this era. One of His best known quotations is "The earth is but one country and mankind its citizens." Who can argue with that? Once we agree there is but one Creator, surely it is clear that there is only one human family. Oneness does not mean sameness; it means unity of mind, feeling and purpose. As Baha'is, our purpose is to bring about the unity of mankind in order to establish "The Most Great Peace."

CHAPTER FOURTEEN

Stephanie and I became the best of friends. When we met, she was taking college courses with the goal of becoming a social worker. I felt envious of her, and shared my disappointment of not having had the opportunity to attend college. She told me it was not too late to get a degree, and encouraged me to start taking courses, as she was doing. Burlington County College was holding classes at Cinnaminson High School. Thus it was, with Stephanie's encouragement, I enrolled in a psych course and acquired my first credits towards a degree. I was forty years old and not sure how long the process would take, nor was I sure of what field I wanted to be my major.

My dilemma was that I was raised in a business environment, and enjoyed the business world. On the other hand, I knew that I had a special bent for the field of human services. At this point, there appeared to be good opportunities for women with solid backgrounds in business administration, while my social worker acquaintances suffered from limited salaries as well as limited job opportunities. After giving it a lot of thought I decided to be "practical" and major in business administration.

I was only able to handle a few courses at a time due to my busy schedule. I not only was busy with the house, and raising the children, I had found a job in a wallpaper showroom and took that on to supplement the family's income. Needless to say, as the boys got older there were lots of expenses that had to be met. I had nearly completed my sixty credits with BCC when it happened.....

My mother was diagnosed with terminal cancer and was sent home from the hospital to spend her last days, as the concept of hospice had not come to fruition yet. We hired someone to care for Mom, but that didn't last long. My headstrong mom got rid of her, claiming she was better off by herself. As her condition worsened, it became apparent she would either have to go to a nursing home, or else move in with me. The malignancy had settled in her spine, and she required round the clock medication and was unable to care for herself. Mom chose the nursing home.

And so it happened that my mother spent the last three months of her life at a nearby nursing home.

I visited with her on an almost daily basis. During these visits I was able to observe and get an overview of what life was like at this facility. It soon became apparent that many of the residents were not suffering from any life-threatening illness, but were more in need of custodial care. Many appeared to be bored, frustrated, and depressed. Their stories touched my heart, and I began to think more and more about the plight of the elderly in our society.

At the store where I worked part time, my boss and I would often chat about things when the showroom was empty. One day the topic turned to my mom. Richard inquired into how she was doing. Then, he fell silent for a moment. I can still picture him as he turned to me and said, "I wonder what life is all about . . . We live for a certain number of years, and then we're gone . . . What does it all mean?"

Although I was knee-deep in business courses at college, there were many opportunities for electives. I found myself taking a number of psychology courses. Recently, one of my assignments had me grapple with the question, "How do you want to be remembered after you're gone?" I had been instructed to write a brief epitaph for my tombstone.

After reflecting on this for a time, I had reached deep inside to come up with an answer, "She made the world just a little bit better."

Now within a short space of time, I was being confronted with the same type of searching question. My prior answer raced through my mind. I didn't actually say anything. It seemed obvious that Richard had asked this query of himself. However, when I got home that evening, I dwelled on the feelings this conversation had evoked. I realized that this could be more than mere rhetoric. After all, I was free to choose the path that I wanted to follow. I could stay on the path I had chosen earlier. This could conceivably lead to the good old "American dream" . . . a prestigious position within the corporate world and all the accompanying perks: the upscale house, late model car, a classy expensive wardrobe, Ivy League colleges for the boys, etc. There was a lot to be said for all that.

However, the more I thought about it, the more I knew I wanted to go in the other direction and try, at least, to make the world "just a little bit better." In my viewpoint, the material goods were not that important when all was said and done, and we looked back in retrospect at our lives.

And so that experience brought me to a turning point in my life. My daily visits to the nursing home had opened my eyes to the problems of the aging population, and the tremendous work that needed to be done in this area. I went on to get my degree in Human Services with a major in Social Gerontology. Upon graduation I was employed as a social worker, working with older adults. The rewards I have received serving in this field are worth more than any material benefits that one could imagine.

CHAPTER FIFTEEN

❧

My days in Cinnaminson were busy, to say the least. I had a large home to care for, and virtually no help from Sandy and the three boys. With Sandy as a role model, they believed that cooking, cleaning and doing laundry was woman's work, as his father before him had professed. Rather than perpetuate constant arguing, it was easier to just do the work myself.

To add to my busy schedule, I was also working part time and taking a few college courses each semester in order to complete my degree. On August 19, 1977, Diane and Stephen became parents of a baby girl, whom they named Ilana. It was so exciting! After all the years raising boys, it was marvelous to welcome a girl to the family.

As the years rolled by, there were many other grandchildren to welcome. After finishing college, David and Larry both married, and each one moved out of state. David competed medical school, and after his residency moved to Maryland, where his wife's family lived. Larry got his degree in marketing and eventually settled in Ohio to be near his wife, Jennifer's family. The last to marry was Michael.

Michael, and his wife, Debera, remain in New Jersey and live in Cherry Hill.

Debera had a high risk pregnancy, and despite being on complete bed rest, gave birth to a boy, Benjamin, three months prematurely. Ben weighed in at only one pound, twelve ounces. Thanks to the medical technology which exists today, he was able to be cared for in the preemie unit where he learned to breathe on his own, and where he gained enough weight to come home to his mom and dad.

Due to the problems Debby faced during pregnancy, the couple decided it would be wise to adopt a child. They became foster parents to a number of children, and then found a nine month old, Andy, who was able to be adopted. Following this, they adopted two other children, Emily and Salena. Their family was now complete. These children were available through DYFS because they were special needs children. Their mothers had been drug addicts, and were not able to care for their newborn infants.

How wonderful to find a home where they were welcomed with open arms.

Today, I have a total of fourteen grandchildren. Since many of them live out of state, I don't get to see them very often. Thankfully, David and Larry call me on a regular basis and keep me informed as to what is happening in their lives.

As I mentioned earlier, I considered the birth of Dave and Larry to be a miracle, since I was so petite at the time they were born. My fervent prayers were answered, as each one came into the world weighing over five pounds. They knew I had prayed for them, and that God had smiled on them and gave them the gift of life.

After graduating high school, Larry enrolled in LaSalle College. Due to problems he was having, he dropped out during his second year. He was supporting himself by selling family portraits in various stores on a commission basis. In 1982 he was doing a photo promotion in Reading, Pennsylvania. He met a couple who befriended him and started asking him a lot of questions. They asked for his name, and soon found out he was Jewish. He observed that there was something different about them, and he was intrigued. He told them he believed in God, but he sensed they were believers in Jesus Christ. He told them he didn't believe in any of "that stuff."

They returned later with a chart about world religions. Larry continued his conversation with them. Eventually, the man challenged him! He asked him to pray to God and ask Him whether Jesus is the Jewish

Messiah. He never saw this couple again, but the events which followed changed his life forever.

Back in his motel room that evening, he turned on the TV. On the screen was Pat Robertson of the 700 Club. He addressed his remarks to the Jews who were watching. What a coincidence! He spoke for a while and then pointed his finger at the viewers and repeated the same words Larry heard earlier in the day.

"I challenge you Jews who are watching to pray to God, and ask him whether Jesus is the Jewish Messiah. What do you have to lose?"

Larry always believed in God, just as I did. So he prayed out loud. He said he wanted to find out if Jesus was alive, like the Gentiles were saying. And he asked for a sign which would reveal the truth. Then he fell asleep.

The next day as he was showering, he heard a voice in his mind. The voice said, "I have come in answer to your prayer." Larry became so unnerved he left the shower and wrapped a towel around himself. He sat on the bed to rest for a moment. Then he said out loud, "How did you come to answer my prayer?"

Once again he heard the voice which said, "What you are looking for is in the mirror."

The room was dark, so he switched on the light....There on the large mirror which he had used for several days, he saw two symbols. He did not recognize them, and did not know what they were. Some time later he learned that the symbols were the

Greek symbols for the Alpha and the Omega, the First and the Last.

After he saw the symbols in the mirror, Larry called me. I still remember the call. I have never heard anyone sound so frightened. The incident had really shaken him up! He couldn't believe what he had heard and then seen with his own eyes. I tried to comfort him. No one could explain the bird who sang to a room full of people the night Clara died. Once you have experienced a mystical happening, you know that such things are possible. The motel manager later verified that the symbols were not there prior to Larry's stay. There is no doubt his prayer had been answered. Although the Baha'i writings do acknowledge psychic phenomena, they make it clear that we are not to try to seek out or develop this type of phenomena.

This incident whet Larry's curiosity about Jesus Christ. He wanted to know more about Him, and thus began reading the Bible. The more he read, the more impact the words carried. Larry says that through the mirror of scripture he found what he had been seeking his whole life, his spiritual identity. He has since published several books which focus on our spirituality. The experience in Reading led him to become a born-again Christian. With each passing year his relationship with the Lord has grown stronger. He is a beautiful example of what a Christian should be. He tries to live a life that exemplifies his beliefs.

The story does not end there. At about the same time this was happening, David was going through a similar transformation. After high school David applied to and was accepted at Lehigh University. As a freshman Dave became friendly with Dwayne and a friend of his. The friend at first was very rowdy, but as the months passed he changed. David did not understand what happened, but accepted it.

The following year the two came to visit Dave in his dorm. They wanted to find out how many students were interested in learning more about Christianity. They had a list of students and asked each one to mark an "i" if interested, and an "n" if not interested. If you were open to hearing a discussion you were asked to put an "o." David put an "o" next to his name.

Eventually, the two came to speak to him, and laid the groundwork for accepting Christ. Later in the year David had to undergo surgery for a testicular torsion, a problem he had probably been born with. Following this, he moved into a fraternity house where Dwayne became his roommate.

Dave told me the following story: One night he fell asleep. While he was sleeping Christ revealed himself, and David said he felt a peace unlike any he had ever experienced. After a while he saw an evil spirit moving toward him. His eyes were blazing and frightening. David did not want anything to do with him. He moved back into the light and felt peaceful again. When he woke up he knew he had met Jesus, and from that moment on accepted him as his Savior.

Although David is a physician he has been through some very hard times. His wife has a chronic, debilitating disease. Two of his four children also suffer from illnesses. Many men would become anxious and depressed under these circumstances. But David says that since the day he accepted Christ into his life, he has been surrounded by peace. In spite of the fact that between work and family he has very little time for himself, he has been working on a Master's degree in Theology. God entered his life through a dream, but for the past thirty years, His presence is always with him and comforts him.

Dave became a Christian just weeks after Larry did. Yet neither one knew the other was contemplating this dramatic change in their lives. They are identical twins who made identical decisions, each one moved by the power of the Spirit.

CHAPTER SIXTEEN

More than four decades have passed since that afternoon in Overbrook Park when my mother and I had lunch together, and she related the dream in which she was told she would be given "the answer." I am only one of countless human beings who has searched for and found the answer to a meaningful existence. The answer, for me, is found in three triangles. I hope it is useful for you, also.

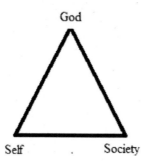

God

Self   .   Society

To start, you yourself must come to realize what a beautiful human being you are. So many of us waste countless hours trying to deal with our feelings of inferiority, or poor self-esteem. I was a prime example of this. The greatest revelation you can make in life is the realization that all people are equal. God made us all different sizes, shapes, and colors, but we are all beautiful human beings. We are the flowers of one garden. Don't you like to see a garden that is full of different colors and varieties of flowers? It is the same with the human race. Celebrate the difference!

Once you have come to realize that you have everything you need to become the person you were meant to be, take some time to evaluate your likes and your talents, and those desires that you hold deep down inside. Then, write down the goals you will need in order to become this great person. Great does not mean that you have to be well-known. It means you love yourself, and believe in yourself, and know you are capable of becoming what you envision in your mind. You can do it, if you believe in yourself. If you do not believe in yourself, no one else will.

Select a career that utilizes the talents that God endowed you with. In my youth I was painfully shy. I did not speak much, but listened a lot to others. Little did I realize that being a good listener was essential to becoming a good social worker. Years later I was grateful that I had developed this skill. Each of us has such a skill. Finding yours is the key to success.

Once you possess the self-confidence you need, you are ready to move on to the next step. Develop positive relationships with the many people who touch your life: your family, your friends, your co-workers, and so on. This is a difficult task and requires much patience. You can pick your friends, but not your relatives. This can be the most difficult thing of all. What do you do with people who do not share your values? We must accept them and try not to judge them. Learning to communicate with others will help you understand where they are coming from, even if you don't agree with them. It is most important to help those in need. Give words of encouragement to others, donate some time to tutor a youngster who needs some extra help, visit an elderly person who has no family nearby, work for an organization like Habitat for Humanity, or the countless other agencies whose aim is to provide assistance to others who need their service. And give whatever money you can to support the work of the many charities that work here at home and abroad. The calendar of the Martin Luther King, Jr. National Memorial says it all. "An individual has not started living until he can rise above the narrow confines of his individualistic concerns to the broader concerns of all humanity." What better person to espouse these words than Dr. King who gave his very life for the cause he believed in.

On Thanksgiving CNN did its annual show on "Heroes." These are ordinary people who have done extraordinary things with their lives. They have found a need sometimes in their back yard and sometimes halfway around the world, and donated a bountiful amount of time and money to help others.

One of the women cited as a hero provides a home and guidance to women who have been released from prison. With her help many women have been able to start a new life and become productive citizens. She said, "All of us have a role and a purpose, and we need to find our purpose."

In case you haven't guessed it, she herself had spent time in prison, and was released with $200.00 as a beginning for the future. She has certainly paid that forward!

"What is the ultimate purpose of life? It is to give." These words were spoken by a chef who quit his well-paying job in a hotel to feed the homeless, the hungry, the ill and the downtrodden. Without his help it is probable that many would die from hunger.

There was a story about a contractor who builds houses for veterans who have been wounded in war. He builds them to be wheel-chair accessible and gives them to our brave men and women for free!! Is this not above and beyond the call of duty? He gives credit to God and says he is simply his instrument.

Many miles away in Kenya there is a young man who has built lanterns for 14,000 children! Without this light the children are unable to do their school work. This is actually reducing the cycle of poverty, because the parents do not have to spend money for kerosene to fuel their kerosene lamps. This young man took on this daunting task and made it his own. He lives his life to serve those in dire need of one simple thing....light.

All ten of the stories were very inspiring. The woman who became "Hero of the Year" lives in India. She saves children from sex trafficking. Her dream is to create a world free from human trafficking. What an enormous, profound dream! And she has spent her life striving for the day this becomes a reality. She was awarded $100,000 to further this cause.

Just a few weeks later Oprah Winfrey had a show which featured Warren Buffet, Bill and Melinda Gates, and Ted Turner. These three men are all billionaires who have given much of the fortunes they have amassed for the betterment of mankind. They have focused on world health with something as simple as vaccines, education in the United States, and the need for nuclear disarmament. Melinda Gates, who runs the Gates Foundation with her husband said, "With great wealth comes great responsibility." They have encouraged other billionaires to sign a "giving pledge" whereby they pledge to give their personal wealth for the betterment of humanity.

I would like to take Mrs. Gates comment one step further. I believe that each of us, regardless of our

as a responsibility to help others in
an. A person who is concerned only
erself, cannot achieve the greatest
ssible. Albert Schweitzer, who is
most brilliant men who ever lived.
know: the only ones among you
appy are those who have sought
ve."

CHAPTER SEVENTEEN

Now it is time to tell you about my own small contribution to society. In my first job as a social worker, I worked in a program under the umbrella of a mental health center. The seniors who attended were suffering from various mental health problems. Many were depressed due to losses they had suffered: the death of a spouse or another loved one; an illness that had lingered over the years, etc. Each participant was placed in a support group that met at least once weekly.

The results were dramatic. As they opened up and shared their feelings and thoughts with others, they bonded with each other, and became like family. They cared about each other, and encouraged each other. The interaction was like a magic potion. Slowly, the depression lifted and they were able to function normally.

They would tell me how much the program helped them. But then, these seniors who were living alone, would have to go home each evening and wait for our program to begin the following day. As the months passed, I began to think about the numerous older adults who had no one to lean on for support. The idea of shared housing began to perk in my mind. Not only would the cost of living be affordable, there would be other folks at hand, with whom to interact each day, to share their stories and other memories.

The idea of shared housing was not new. Maggie Kuhn, head of Gray Panthers, had pioneered the idea in Philadelphia. At the time I worked at the mental health center, I belonged to the Unitarian Church in Cherry Hill. The church was very much involved in social action projects. We invited Maggie Kuhn to speak at our church, and I introduced her and spoke about the project which I envisioned.

One of the church members gave a wine and cheese social gathering at his home which was used as a fund raiser. We put together a Board which would become active when we incorporated. The name ALLY was chosen for the corporation. The dictionary defines ALLY as "people working together for a common cause." This seemed very appropriate. The actual name is Alternative Living for Later Years.

The proposed agency was given news coverage in the local papers. A Lutheran minister and his wife expressed interest in the project and were asked to join the ALLY board. Through this minister's efforts we received a $500.00 grant from Lutheran Social Services. With the money we hired an attorney, incorporated in New Jersey, and obtained a 501(c)3 from Internal Revenue. My dream was about to become a reality.

I started exploring where one could find grant money for such a project. In Trenton, the state's capital, I located the headquarters of the Housing Demonstration Program. When I contacted them I was invited to tell them of our idea, which at the time was unique in New Jersey. Several of us made the trek to Trenton where we explained our concept which would provide affordable housing to low income seniors. It had become difficult for the elderly to maintain their homes with taxes escalating every year, and the cost of maintenance climbing as well.

The gentleman who headed the program agreed it was a worthwhile project. We were told that when we found a suitable property, we would need to fund fifty percent of the residence, and the Housing Demonstration Program would provide the additional fifty percent that was needed.

ALLY became incorporated in 1984, and two years later we found a four bedroom, two bath ranch home in Cinnaminson, New Jersey. The rancher was ideally located near a bank and a shopping center which was within walking distance. The owners were willing to take back a mortgage on the property, but we needed an additional twenty thousand dollars to reach our goal of fifty percent down.

One evening, as I arrived home from work, I received a call from the person who was working as our financial advisor. He informed me there was a meeting that evening in Moorestown, to explore the township's options regarding affordable housing. Each town state-wide had been asked to set aside a number of properties to be built or acquired for those in need of this type of housing.

I had been working all week and felt really tired and didn't want to go, so I politely declined. Our advisor, Mr. Bryant, told me it was an important meeting and he felt strongly that we should be in attendance. Therefore, we made arrangements to meet and go together. As we entered the Town Hall they asked those who wished to speak on the topic to sign up. I had nothing in mind, and thought it would be better to just listen.

About a half hour into the meeting, several residents spoke about the large homes that were available in Moorestown, and they expressed an interest in the idea of utilizing these homes as shared housing. This seemed like a perfect opportunity to bring up ALLY, and at this point I asked to address the audience. I informed the onlookers that ALLY was a non-profit organization which had recently been incorporated, and was now prepared to purchase and operate shared housing. After I spoke several people approached me and asked for information about ALLY.

The next day, to my surprise, the Courier Post ran a piece about the meeting, and the heading read, "ALLY Proposes Shared Housing." Later in the day I received a phone call from someone who had seen the article and wanted to know more about our organization. We decided to meet for lunch so we could discuss the idea further.

As we talked over lunch the next day I mentioned the house we had recently found for sale in Cinnaminson. My new acquaintance asked if we were planning to buy it. I explained we were twenty thousand dollars short of being able to close the deal. What happened next will remain in my consciousness for the rest of my life. This woman, whom I had never met, or even heard of, said she would lend us the money for a two year period, and charge us only a modest amount of interest.

To say I was amazed would be the understatement of our time. It turned out Marian Steininger was a well-known philanthropist in our area. The Steininger Mental Health Center in Camden County was named for her husband. This generous offer from someone I had just met enabled ALLY to go forward and purchase its first property. Years later, I am at a loss to be able to explain in realistic terms how this had come about.

Simply stated, I reluctantly attended a meeting I didn't want to attend, listened to statements about shared housing I had no idea would come forth, and made a brief announcement about ALLY and its support of affordable housing. Consequently, we ended up with a check for twenty thousand dollars. How could this be? Nowhere in my wildest dreams could I have envisioned this scenario.

This brings me to the third, and highest point, on the triangle: belief in God. What happened was nothing I was capable of planning. Yes, we had found a house, and I had explored funding options, but the rest of the scenario is nothing short of a miracle. You don't believe in miracles? Well, neither did I until the night that Clara died. The bird that chirped in my living room that night was a forerunner of things that are not of this world. There are things we cannot see or understand, but they are real, nevertheless.

Faith in God can accomplish miracles. It is my belief that if you lead a good life, love, and feel compassion for others God will help you accomplish the goals you have set to help others. Without faith ALLY would never have been formed. Each of us can make a difference in the world. Dream the dream, and take whatever steps you can to help others, and you will be rewarded many times over for your efforts. ALLY eventually owned and operated three residences in South Jersey for a period of twenty-five years. When the time came for me to retire, I was able to turn the organization over to another non-profit housing group which was headed by a Presbyterian minister. But none of this could have happened without God's mercy. I am forever grateful for His help in overcoming the many hurdles along the way.

CHAPTER EIGHTEEN

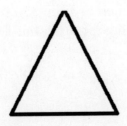

The second triangle goes into greater detail about how one develops into a happy, healthy, well-functioning human being. There are many factors which must be considered.

Spiritual

Physical   Mental/Emotional

Let's start with physical well-being:

We are born with DNA which we inherited from our parents. We can't do anything about that, but there is much we can do to enable our bodies to function at an optimal level.

One of the most important ways we can nourish our bodies is to eat a healthy, well-balanced diet. There are volumes written on how to achieve a healthy diet. Acquaint yourself with the Food Pyramid. That is where you must start. After reviewing the data, try to slowly move to healthier food choices over time. Through force of habit, many of us eat things that are not good for us: fried foods, processed food, red meat, too much salt, too much sugar and refined grains. We don't consume enough whole grains, fresh fruits and vegetables, and ample servings of fish which contain omega-3 fish oils, like salmon.

Interestingly enough, I have seen many elderly people complain about their health, but think nothing of shoving junk food into their mouths, and never think about the correlation that exists between diet and good health. We may know that certain things are good for us, but we must be able to go to the next level and enforce our knowledge with action. If we continue to make poor choices, there is no one to blame but ourselves. Feed your body what it needs, and it will continue to serve you for many years to come.

I am a big believer in vitamin supplements, even though there are diverse opinions on this topic. Since age thirty I have taken a high potency multi-vitamin, and a combination Vitamin B and C tablet which is good for stress. It has been said you can't overdose on these two vitamins since they are water soluble, and your body will dispose of the excess. For the last year I have also taken reservatrol, one of the ingredients in red wine. It has been proven to provide antioxidant protection by fighting the effects of free radicals.

Just as important as good nutrition is getting regular exercise. For many years I belonged to a gym and did both aerobic exercise and used weight-bearing machines. There are also an assortment of videos that can be used. Again, people come up with every imaginable excuse for not exercising. It is important to speak to your doctor if you have not exercised. Ask your doctor what type of exercise to do, how often, and how long. Unless he or she tells you not to exercise, then find an exercise program and join it, if you can.

It has been established that a good goal for most of us is to exercise at least three times a week, for thirty to sixty minutes at a time. But if you have not been exercising it is best to start out slowly. The benefits of regular exercise are numerous:

- Keeps joints, tendons and ligaments flexible
- Reduces your risk of heart disease, high blood pressure, osteoporosis, diabetes and obesity
- Helps relieve stress and anxiety
- Contributes to your mental well-being and helps treat depression
- Helps you sleep better

- Increases your metabolism which helps you maintain a normal weight[1]

Set up an exercise schedule and stick to it. Once you get in the habit of exercising, you will find you feel good when you are done. It is well worth the effort. Aerobic exercise improves the health of your heart and lungs. It includes walking, jogging, dancing, bicycling, etc. Weight-bearing exercise works against the force of gravity. It is important in building strong bones. If you want to prevent osteoporosis and bone fractures later in life, include weight-bearing exercise in your workout.

Let's move on to mental/emotional health.

Just as there are things you can do to stay healthy physically, there are a number of things you can do to be healthy mentally and emotionally. We have already covered the importance eating a healthy diet, and getting regular exercise. Both of these items contribute significantly to your mental well-being. All the more reason to be diligent in your eating habits, and staying active physically. Exercise can enhance your mood, leaving you feeling relaxed.

Be sure you get enough sleep. Experts suggest that adults get seven to nine hours of sleep at night. Indeed, poor sleep has been linked to significant problems:

- Greater risk of depression and anxiety

- Impaired memory

- Increased risk of heart disease and cancer

- Reduced functioning of our immune system
- Greater likelihood of accidents[2]

Another important factor is being connected to others. Humans are social beings. We need to feel supported, valued, loved, and connected to other people. Family is important, but friends and co-workers also play a big role. In one recent study good relationships were found to be the key difference between very happy people and those who were less happy.

I can't emphasize enough the importance of being positive. This is a proven way to feel stronger and more hopeful. People who are pessimistic have been found to have a higher risk of dying than those who are optimistic. Many years ago I took a workshop entitled "Adventures in Attitudes." This program dramatically changed my life. I learned how to gain control and mastery over my thoughts so that I was able to accomplish what I wanted to do with my life. It gave me the confidence to go forward and establish the non-profit group, ALLY, which became the cornerstone of my existence.

Although Adventures in Attitudes is no longer in existence, there are similar programs available, and numerous self-help books on the shelves to help you understand the importance of how you think. You must think positive thoughts if you want to accomplish your goals in life. You can overcome any negative thoughts you may have. If you believe it, you can do it. That dream you have can become a reality. I am living proof of that.

We already touched on the importance of helping others. On the website "Mental Health America," it states that "research indicates that those who consistently help other people experience less depression, greater calm, fewer pains and better health."[3] What more of an incentive could you have?

Indeed, doing good for others does render many benefits. It can help you feel needed and effective, as well as add a sense of purpose to your life. It is a wonderful feeling to know you have been able to help others. There are a myriad of ways you can volunteer your service. Find an organization that interests you and give them a call. Any time you can give will be a blessing.

Leave time in your life for joy. Make sure you fit in some leisure activities. If you enjoy golf, or tennis, or shooting hoops, for instance, indulging in this activity will give you great satisfaction. Play games that you enjoy. I am a big Scrabble buff, and I play on-line and in person on a regular basis. The same goes for card games and puzzles and reading. And if music is your passion, indulge yourself as often as you can, either by playing an instrument or listening to your favorite CDs. You can listen to your favorite symphony, or hear that artist who brings a big smile to your face.

What to do when you're upset:

If you've experienced something upsetting, it can be very helpful to speak to a close friend or relative. You may also want to consider speaking to a minister or rabbi. Many have good counseling skills. Speaking about ongoing problems will give you an emotional release. Keeping problems pent up is the worst thing you can do. It can lead to severe physical problems.

If you don't have anyone to talk to, write about it. Don't worry about grammar or spelling. Just spill out what the problem is and how it has made you feel. If you are going through a prolonged period of stress you might want to consider keeping a journal. Be sure to put in the positive things that happen also.

Lastly, if you are dealing with something that is truly disturbing, I would recommend getting help from a therapist. There is nothing to be ashamed of in asking for help. Getting professional assistance will help you deal with the problems you are facing. It will reduce your anxiety and enable you to function in a normal capacity.

CHAPTER NINETEEN

At the top of our triangle is spirituality. Being spiritual relates to, or consists of, our inner spirit, not things tangible or material. Spiritual growth is not the same as being religious. Religion, over time, often becomes encrusted with human-made ideas and practices. Godly spirituality does not come from what man has dictated, but from true and earnest desires of the heart.

Spiritual people generally believe in:

- Prayer (regularly conversing with God.)
- Becoming students of His Word and teachings
- Sharing the blessings of spirituality with others

- Giving glory to God through words and behavior

When we grow spiritually we will draw closer to the Lord. This gives us a joy and peace in life that defies all circumstances. Ultimately, we come to understand and appreciate the many blessings the Lord has bestowed on us.

What makes someone spiritual? In my own life, I always believed in God, so the many experiences that followed simply reinforced what I had always known. But what about those who do not believe? In this age of technology we can find the answer to almost anything on the internet. So I plugged "the existence of God" into my search engine. I found a very interesting piece by Marilyn Adamson. Ms. Adamson states she had been an atheist and was bothered by the idea that people believed in God. She felt such people were delusional. She also wanted to prove that these believers were wrong.

Later, she came to realize that the reason that this topic was weighing on her mind was because God wants to be known, and he causes this issue to be on our minds and, therefore, search for the answer. Her web site offers six reasons that offer proof of His existence:

- The complexity of our planet
- The universe had its start with what scientists now call the Big Bang theory
- The universe operates by uniform laws of nature

- The DNA code informs and programs a cell's behavior

- He pursues those who are searching for Him

- For Christians the proof is in the life of Jesus Christ. It is a clear picture of God revealing himself to us4

For those of you who are interested, all of the above reasons are discussed at length on Ms. Adamson's website. She states that after a year of questioning, she responded to God's offer to come into her life and has found faith in Him to be "constantly substantial and greatly rewarding."

Another interesting person is Dr. Elisabeth Kubler-Ross, the Swiss born psychiatrist and author who gained international fame for her ground-breaking work in the field of death and dying. She has written several books on the subject. After years of researching the topic of Near Death Experiences she came to the conclusion that death does not exist.

She says her most unforgettable case was a man who was to be picked up by his family for a Memorial Day weekend. The van they were driving in was hit by a gasoline tanker, and his entire family was killed. This included his wife, her parents, and his eight children. In just an instant every person in his family was wiped out.

To ease the pain he started drinking and tried heroin and other drugs. He was not able to hold a job and ended up in the gutter. Dr. Kubler-Ross had finished two lectures in one day and was asked to do another. She was bored with repeating the same stories to her audience. So she prayed a silent prayer, "Oh God, why don't you send me someone who has had a NDE and is willing to share it with the audience?"

At the very moment she finished her prayer someone gave her a slip of paper. It was a message from a man from the bowery who wanted to share his NDE with her. She sent a cab to pick him up, and a short while later he showed up. Without a chance to interview him, he was asked to go on stage and share his story.

He told about the accident which had burned his family to death, and the shock and numbness of losing everyone, including his children. He drank every day from morning to night, used drugs, and tried to commit suicide several times, but was not able to succeed. Of course, he was not able to work. After two years of this life style, he recalls lying on a dirt road, drunk and stoned. He did not even have the energy to move out of the road when he saw a big truck approaching. The truck ran over him.

He left his body, and while critically injured, watched the entire scene from a few feet above. At that moment his family appeared in front of him in a glow of light, with an incredible sense of love. They had broad smiles on their faces, did not communicate verbally, but through thought transference shared with him the joy and happiness of their present existence. He was awed by his family's health and radiance. He made a vow not to join them, but to reenter his physical body, so that he could share with the world what he had experienced. It would be an act of redemption for the two years he had thrown away.

An ambulance sped him to the emergency room. He re-entered his body, tore off the straps around him and literally walked out of the E.R. He did not have any after effects from the heavy abuse of drugs and alcohol. Instead, he felt healed. He vowed he would not die until he shared his experience with as many people as would listen. He had gained the awareness that our physical body is only the shell that encloses our immortal self.

Dr. Kubler-Ross says, "After your death, most of you will for the first time realize what life is all about. You will begin to see that your life here is the sum total of every choice you have made. Your thoughts, which you are responsible for, are as real as your deeds. You will realize that every word and deed affects your life, and has also touched the lives of many others."[5]

Believing in God, and going to church or synagogue or mosque is not enough. You must try to be kind and caring and compassionate with every breath you take. Love everyone, even those who are not so lovable. They may have gone through hard times and may need your love even more than others. It is easy to love someone who has been kind, but more difficult to care about someone who has been abusive. You should not put up with abuse, but you need not react in kind. That is why I believe children should not be hit. They grow up believing it is OK to hit someone if they don't like what is said or done to them. Children need structure and discipline, but there are loving ways to enforce discipline. The same is true for shouting at them, and demeaning them. The harm you can do by constantly berating a child can last a lifetime. They need love and encouragement. You can give it to them. It can shape their entire lives in a positive way.

Lastly, when you need help, reach out to God. He is always there when you need His support. Thank Him every day for all the blessings he has bestowed on you. Accept people of all religions. God does not endorse any one religion. He loves everyone who honors Him and lives his or her life to spread joy and kindness to those with whom they come in contact. This is indeed a challenge, but we need to work on becoming God's emissary in this world. It is a lifelong task. We are never finished.

My son, Larry, has lived his adult life as a spiritual being. He has his own web site at brotherlarry.com, and within this web site offers a daily reflection and prayer. If you need help with bringing about your purpose in life, you may want to pray the following prayer which Larry has suggested:

"Lord, thank you for eternal purpose that brings dividends for a sure blessing. Help me to realize both my general and specific purpose to serve you in the best possible way. Amen."[6]

CHAPTER TWENTY

In time, the years will roll by, and one day you find yourself in the later years of your life. Where did those prior years go? What are you supposed to do? The children are now grown and are living their lives elsewhere. Your working days have ended and you face an endless stretch of time known as retirement. And for many of us we are divorced or widowed and living alone. Moreover, we realize the house we have lived in for umpteen years is way too big for our needs, and way too expensive to maintain. It's time for a whole new lifestyle.

Let's look at triangle number three.

Successful Aging

Senior You

(Mind/Body/Spirit)

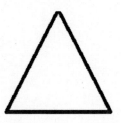

Relationships   Living Accommodations

Let's begin by examining your life during these senior years. As we described earlier, diet and exercise play an important role in your well-being. This continues to be true as you age. Eating healthy food and staying away from unhealthy choices have a direct impact on your health. The same is true with exercise. A study posted in the Journal of Aging and Health found that women over 85 who exercise four hours per week have a 88% decreased risk of cognitive impairment![7] That's mind boggling!!

The reason is that physical activity challenges your brain and forces it to learn new movements and skills. Think of the brain as a muscle. The more you use it, the stronger it becomes. Yet many senior citizens do not engage in adequate exercise. Most senior centers throughout the country do make exercise programs available. It is important to recognize that exercise and diet is vital for your continuing health. The choice is yours.

All through life, but especially in your senior years, you want to maintain good mental health. This can be difficult, for sure. The elderly person often faces many losses. Among them is the loss of health, mobility, independence, career, and especially the loss of a loved one. Loss is painful, and grieving over these losses is normal for a period of time. However, losing all hope and joy is not a normal part of aging.

Depression is a serious concern, because untreated it can lead to suicide. A little known fact is that the elderly are the highest risk population in our country for suicide. The overall suicide rate in the U.S. is 11 per 100,000 people. For those 65 and older, the figure rises to 14 per 100,000. Older adults are less likely to seek help, and are more lethal in their suicide attempts. It is, indeed, a very serious problem.[8]

Moreover, with treatment and support depressed seniors can feel better. There is no need to live with depression. Here are some tips for battling this disease:

- Stay connected to others
- Find activities you enjoy, and participate in them
- Pursue hobbies that interest you
- Attend classes on topics that interest you
- Volunteer some of your time at your local school or hospital

- Go to your local SPCA and adopt a pet to keep you company

- If you have not done so previously, learn how to meditate

- Join a gym and exercise, or walk outside on a regular basis

Remember, the more active you are—physically, mentally and socially—the better you will feel. Some medications can trigger depression, so be sure to tell your physician if you find you are depressed. And as stated earlier, if you are so depressed that you don't want to go anywhere, or do anything, or if you think about suicide, please seek professional help. Having a mental illness is no different than having a physical illness. There is help available if you reach out for it. Life is too precious to be spent feeling down in the dumps for a long period of time.

Maintaining relationships, or starting new ones, is important to your well-being as you advance in age. Being isolated is a major factor leading to depression and other problems. If you have siblings or children living nearby, try to visit with them, or eat lunch or dinner with them on a regular basis. If family members live further away, keep in touch via telephone.

Try to establish new relationships, also. Visit your local senior community center and check out their schedule of activities. If you don't drive, sign up for bus service, so that you can be transported there, and other necessary places.

In Haddonfield, New Jersey, retired men in that community formed a "65 Club." In addition to guest speakers and varied activities, plus special events, many of the members volunteer their services to local organizations. The club has posted on-line their Philosophy of Life. I would like to share it with you.

"Youth is not a time of life—it is a state of mind. Nobody grows old by merely living a number of years. Years wrinkle the skin, but to give up enthusiasm wrinkles the soul. Worry, doubt, self-distrust, fear and despair—these are the long, long years that bow the head and turn the growing spirit back to dust. Whether seventy or sixteen, there is in every being's heart the love of wonder, the sweet amazement at the stars, the undaunted challenge of events, the unfailing childlike appetite for what's next, and the joy of the game of life."[9]

This club is a prime example of helping older adults maintain the joy that is available as we stroll through our elder years. Joy is there for us to reach out and embrace if we make a decision to make it a part of our ongoing existence.

One of the most important decision seniors have to make is where we will live. There are many options available, and there is no "one size fits all" answer. We are all unique and have many varied circumstances. There are several important factors to consider. First, and possibly foremost, is our health. Secondly we have to be guided by our financial resources. Naturally, the person whose income is limited has far less choices available.

Let's start at the beginning. For folks with low and moderate incomes, the Federal government has a program in place known as Section 8 Housing. Since funding for this has been cut back in recent years, there is a waiting list for most Section 8 units. You can put your name on a waiting list and wait for an opening to come up. When it does, you will pay 30% of your monthly income for an apartment, and the government, through HUD, pays the balance. Use the internet to help you find affordable housing.

A second option is to explore Retirement Living Communities. Each community has a minimum age requirement. You can use the money from the sale of your house to purchase a home in such a community. You will be able to live with other seniors with whom you can form friendships. There is generally a club house where there are ongoing activities, and often a fitness center. They advertise in senior magazines, local newspapers, and once again check online or have someone do that for you.

If you can afford to move into a retirement community which offers apartment units, this is a good way to meet and interact with other like-minded senior citizens. These communities usually offer meals and housekeeping services. You need to determine the type of community that will best serve your needs and your pocketbook. Do you need independent living or require assisted living? The latter will be more expensive. A step upward are Continuing Care and Life Care communities. These type of communities generally require an entrance fee which can be substantial. However, you will be cared for as your needs change, and you will not have to move elsewhere if you become infirm. Check out their charges carefully.

For those who have chosen not to move, and find themselves needing help because of their frail health, there is Home Care available through a wide array of Home Care agencies. Some available services may be covered under Medicare, Medicaid, and Veterans Administration. However, some, or all of the cost may have to be paid out of pocket. If you live alone, this lifestyle will not provide the social interaction that is extremely important to your well-being. Therefore, I believe that aging in-place should only be considered as a last resort.

Spend all the time you need to check out what is available. Make phone inquiries, ask for brochures, and, of course, visit in person. If possible, spend a week or two as a guest in a facility. That is the best way to ascertain what living there will be like.

CHAPTER TWENTY-ONE

My story began in 1930 when several relatives who had departed this world came to visit my mother in a dream. They prophesized that my mother was to be given "the answer." Very shortly thereafter mom realized that she was carrying me in her womb. Now, some eighty years later, I have been able to come to visualize what "the answer" is. This knowledge did not come to me all at once, but slowly, step by step, year by year, the realization has grown in my heart and soul. It is now time to share it with you.

My life has been fairly traditional. It has had its ups and downs, pretty much the same as everyone else who lives. The lessons I have learned through life experiences were actually highlighted and summed up in the form of three triangles. These triangles, when superimposed on each other, form a nine-pointed star, which is the symbol of the Baha'i Faith.

The search, which began early in my youth, and continued over many decades ended with this nine-pointed star. There is no doubt in my mind that this is the answer which has been given to me by God. It is, indeed, also the answer to world peace. Peace cannot be achieved by the dictates of one country or one world leader. It must come about through the consciousness of multitudes of men and women who have first loved themselves, and then extended this love to the balance of mankind.

The Baha'i Faith has become an integral part of my life and provided me with a wealth of peace and tranquility, because it is such a positive force for good in the world. At the present time we live in a world where warfare and violence is still taking place. Although each major religion calls for peace among its people, extremists perpetuate hatred for those who do not embrace their own religion. Many brave young men and women have been killed, and thousands more have been wounded physically and mentally as they fight to protect us from these extremists who would do us harm.

The extremists are misguided individuals who have used their own sacred writings to justify their actions. In reality, the Scriptures of all major religions profess love, harmony and peace. But, unfortunately, they are subject to interpretation. There are too many among us who believe that their religion is the only right way.

Baha'is, like myself, believe that since the days of Adam God has sent a series of Divine Messengers who have become founders of separate religions, but whose common goal has been to bring the human race to spiritual and moral maturity. We still have a long road to travel, but with every passing year we have a growing number of people whose consciousness has been raised so that they embrace peace for themselves, and project it forward into the universe.

Today, the Baha'i Faith is among the fastest growing religions in the world. They have established significant communities in more than 100 countries. This is more than any other religion, except Christianity. There are currently millions of members who've come from virtually every nationality, religious background, ethnic group and social class. It is the greatest unifying force that exists today. Many people have come to realize, as I do, that religions are not meant to compete with each other, and that one religion is not better than another. Just as we have to accept each other as individuals, we have to accept that all religions are meant to live in harmony with each other. I have attended a number of interfaith programs, and there is nothing more uplifting than attending services with my neighbors of all faiths and denominations.

Baha'i principles include:

- the oneness of humankind
- the equality of men and women
- the abandonment of all forms of prejudice
- the realization of universal education
- eliminating the extremes of poverty and wealth
- the establishment of a global commonwealth of nations
- recognizing that religion is in harmony with reason and the pursuit of science

His Holiness, the Dalai Lama, a Tibetan Buddhist, wrote in 2002: "Internal peace is an essential first step to achieving peace in the world. How do you cultivate it? It is very simple. In the first place by realizing clearly that all mankind is one, that human beings in every country are one and the same family."

Indeed, this is the same message echoed by Baha'i Faith. From a Baha'i perspective, none of this is coincidental. We are living in a new age, opened with the Revelation of Baha'u'llah. There are many positive developments which are the reflections of the new movement toward global peace and unity. Indeed, there are many groups working toward peace and promoting human rights. The Peace Alliance and Amnesty International are just two who are leading the charge.

There are people in other countries who are being incarcerated and even executed because they are speaking out for freedom. We must raise our voices in opposition to this brutality. We must offer whatever support we can by our messages and donating whatever we can to the cause. It is important to remember that none of us will be really free until all of us are free.

We don't have to look overseas in order to find a huge infringement to our safety and well-being taking place. On January 8, 2011, Americans were horrified to learn of the shooting which took place in Tucson, Arizona, which took six innocent lives, including a nine year old girl, and the wounding of thirteen others, including Congresswoman Gabrielle Giffords.

Since then we've gone back to the debate which has been raging in our country for many years. Yes, the Second Amendment to the Constitution gives us the right to bear arms. I'd like to remind everyone reading this that 1776 was a different era. The law, which made sense then, does more harm than good to those of us living in the twenty-first century. Other laws have changed. Parents who used to beat their children are no longer allowed to do that. But gun control is a sacred cow which can't be changed, thanks to the NRA which is heavily invested in the issue.

Christine Green, the nine year old girl who was killed in Tucson, was so proud of living in this country that she wanted to meet Congresswoman Giffords and follow her example. Due to the act of a deranged individual, her life was snuffed out. Was the right of her assailant to carry a weapon more important than Christine's right to grow up and follow her dreams? I have never understood this debate. Except for a handful of people who own a business and have stashed a gun under the counter for protection, I rarely hear of anyone who was able to pull out a gun and use it to defend themselves. While the hypothesis makes sense, the reality doesn't.

During the multiple attacks by terrorists on September 11, 2001, over three thousand people were killed. It was a terrible day in our nation's history. And citizens throughout the country spoke out vehemently against al-Qaeda who sponsored these attacks on so many innocent people. Yet in 2007 there were over twelve thousand murders committed by firearms, and another 613 persons were killed unintentionally.[10] Did you hear any mention of this in the news? I didn't. Furthermore, of the more than two hundred thousand people who were homicide victims between 1988 and 1997, sixty-eight percent of the victims were killed with guns. Does this sound like we're on the road to peace? If we have four times as many people killed within one year by gunfire as were killed on 9/11, why is this acceptable?

This country is riddled with violence. What is the answer? We need to acknowledge that prejudice, war, violence, and exploitation are signs of immaturity in our long historical process. Just as children go through stages of immaturity before they reach adulthood, so, too, do nations.

The Declaration of Independence gave this nation a vision for the future, and declared its citizens had the right to "Life, Liberty, and the Pursuit of Happiness." America's founders put forth a bright vision for us to embrace. Now, at the beginning of the twenty-first century it is time that our citizens examine our moral principles, and ponder how to establish an institution which will foster peace and tranquility both here and abroad.

CHAPTER TWENTY-TWO

❧❧

During the last century more than one hundred million people died in wars. Isn't it time we said, "enough violence," and begin to establish a culture of peace? It is time to conceive of peace as not simply the absence of violence, but the presence of a higher evolution of the human awareness....which includes respect, trust and integrity.

Ten years ago legislation was introduced into the United States House of Representatives whose aim was to create a Department of Peace. HR 808 has been re-introduced in the 112th Congress. This legislation will accomplish the following:

- Establish a cabinet-level department in the executive branch of the Federal Government dedicated to peacemaking and the study of conditions that are conducive to both domestic and international peace.

- It will be headed by a Secretary of Peace and Nonviolence to be appointed by the President.

- The mission of the Department shall be to strengthen nonmilitary means of peacemaking, and develop policies that promote national and international conflict prevention.

- Domestically, the Department would be responsible for developing policies to address such issues as: domestic violence, gang violence, child abuse, violence in schools, hate crimes, racial violence and mistreatment of the elderly.

- The Office of Peace Education would work with educators to develop and implement curricula to instruct students in peaceful conflict resolution skills.

- January 1st will be designated as Peace Day in the United States. Citizens will be encouraged to celebrate the blessings of peace and endeavor to create peace in the coming year.[11]

It is clear in reading the above summary that the concept of a Department of Peace has been well thought out, and will provide a significant start to establishing peace, both here at home as well as abroad. And peace is cost effective! Reducing violence by 3% would pay for a U.S. Department of Peace, and ultimately save many lives. The United States is well recognized as a world leader. It would be most appropriate to become the leader in this long overdue quest for world peace.

Resolutions supporting the concept have been passed by the governing bodies of 35 city, county and other local administrations including: Atlanta, Chicago, Detroit, Los Angeles and San Francisco. These entities represent approximately 12.5 million people. In addition, it has been endorsed by over 50 organizations, including Amnesty International, NOW and Physicians for Social Responsibility.

There already exists a Global Alliance for Ministries and Departments of Peace.

The Global Alliance is a civil society organization calling for the establishment of Ministries and Departments of Peace in governments worldwide! There are currently 40 member countries, with the newest member being South Sudan. It is time for America to become a part of this movement.

Hopefully, one day in the not too distant future, when things settle down in the nation's capitol, when our elected officials put aside their personal aspirations and turn their focus on working for the common good of their constituents, the bill for creating a Department of Peace may come up for consideration. In the meantime, spread the word to those you know, and write a letter to your Congressman and Senator voicing your support for this concept. Right now, it is only a dream, but with massive grassroots support from citizens on both sides of the isle, victory can be achieved. It is certainly a concept that will be able to produce positive changes in our nation as we take on the challenge of peace.

CHAPTER TWENTY-THREE

❧❧

While we are waiting, there is much we can do as individuals. I have just finished reading *The Twelfth Insight* by James Redfield. It is a fascinating story based on the prophecy of the Mayan people that projects the world will end in December of 2012. Mr. Redfield explains that this does not mean that Armageddon will take place. Yes, if we continue on the path of violence which has become very prolific over the past decade, there is definitely a possibility that eventually the earth will be destroyed. However, the alternative is for the world to end . . . as we know it. In that instance the violence and brutality which we have witnessed via our television sets, can be replaced with an era which Baha'is refer to as "The Most Great Peace."

Albeit that our nightly news programs are chock full of stories of bombings and shootings and torture being inflicted by despotic rulers plus crazed individuals who go on a killing spree, there is something else going on which is not being broadcast. That something else is a "raised consciousness" by large groups of people. In the midst of this something marvelous is being created. The group involved as a whole discovers that the individuals are greater than their parts. Their intelligence and capacity far exceeds what would be expected of them! Craig Hamilton has written about this in a document called "Come Together." It is truly inspiring.

Robert Kenny and Carol Frenier have researched and documented this type of collective consciousness. Although this social dynamic has been known to exist for the past decade, it has just recently come to the forefront where it has been acknowledged. The internet shows many thousand results for terms like "collective consciousness" and "group mind." The possibilities that may emerge from this collective awakening are considered to be revolutionary.

Ken Keyes, Jr. says in his book *Power of Unconditional Love*, "The social cooperativeness that flows when we love everyone as a brother or sister is needed to help solve the immense planetary problems we have created."

The question is, "How do we get there?" A good place to start is by looking into an interfaith initiative. Being able to accept all of the world's religions would be a giant step toward establishing peace and harmony. Mahatma Gandhi has said the following: "Like the bee gathering honey from the different flowers, the wise person accepts the essence of the different scriptures, and sees only the good in all religions." Study the different religions, and you will find that each one projects peace and love to the world in which we live.

The United Religious Initiative was established to promote enduring, daily interfaith cooperation, to end religiously motivated violence, and to create cultures of peace, justice and healing for the Earth and all living beings. The organization has its global office in San Francisco, California, and is active in 78 countries. They have a network of 514 interfaith Cooperation Circles throughout the world and include half a million members.[12] They engage people of different faiths to work together for the good of their communities. It is a beautiful idea, but unfortunately you don't hear about this type of spiritual enterprise on the evening news. The news of the day focuses mainly on violence. No wonder so many people are depressed with the state of our world!!

In April, 2011, there was an International Seminar on Religions for Peace and Harmony held at the University of Dhaka in Bangladesh.[13] This university has been very active in trying to promote and strengthen the movement of inter-religious dialogue. Professor Arefin Siddique, Vice chancellor of the university, reaffirmed that each religion urges us to love one another as shown by the Golden Rule. Professor Siddique joins a multitude of voices which note that since the core of each religion puts forth the

127

philosophy of love, respect, and non-violence, it is important for all religions to cooperate in order to bring forth a new culture of peace.

However, this is not an easy task. We are aware that many Muslim extremists, ignorant of the true teachings of their religion, have killed scores of innocent people in recent months. But there are also Christian extremists. The minister who burned the Quran to show his displeasure of Muslims, did a tremendous disservice to his Christian faith. And the Norwegian who set off a bomb in Oslo, Norway, and then went on to shoot over sixty innocent children on a nearby island, considers himself a Christian. He purportedly was worried about the impact of a large number of Muslims moving into and impacting Europe.

While these men can clearly be labeled as extremists, there are an untold number of fundamentalist Christians who hold the rigid view as purported in the Bible, that only those who believe in Christ will receive salvation and go on to live with God upon their death here on earth. That means that millions of Hindus, Muslims and Jews, and people of other faiths who believe in God and have worshipped Him within their own culture, will not enjoy an afterlife with their heavenly Father. Nevertheless, I do believe that everyone who loves God, and worships God and tries to lead an exemplary life here on earth, will someday meet their Maker, and I am certainly not alone in this belief.

Christians that I know have said that the Quran talks a lot about jihad, and encourages violence.

However, the Bible also contains passages which contradict peace.

In Matthew 10:32 Christ says, "Whoever acknowledges me before men, I will also acknowledge him before my Father in heaven. But whoever disowns me before men, I will disown Him before my Father in heaven. Do not suppose that I have come to bring peace to earth, but a sword."

When Joshua and his followers conquered Jericho, they killed everyone who lived there with the exception of Rahab. She had hidden and protected the spies who had been sent there. Joshua went on to attack other communities, also. Does this sound like a peaceful way to solve a problem?

The question that arises from this back and forth finger pointing at holy scriptures is this: Are the Bible and other scriptures meant to be taken literally? Again, I headed to the internet in search of an answer. I spent several hours reading the thoughts of learned men and women, and found persuasive arguments both pro and con. Just when I thought there would be no answer, I came across a two page article written by a gentleman I had never heard of. His name was Emanuel Swedenborg. What makes this man believable is that he was an absolutely brilliant scientist and physicist who was way ahead of his time in his thinking. He was also an expert in mine engineering, metallurgy, astronomy and political economics. When he was 55 his life began to change. This man who had had an intellectual approach to life, began having dreams and psychical experiences. He developed spiritual insights and wrote several volumes based on these insights.

Just as I believed Larry when he saw the Alpha and Omega in the mirror of his motel room, after reading Swedenborg's biography, I did believe that his revelations were inspired from a Higher Source. One of his purposes was to reveal an inner meaning of the Bible. Swedenborg suggests that the literal sense of the Bible is merely the container for an inner, spiritual sense. He writes in his book *Heavenly Secrets*: "As long as the mind confines itself to the sense of the literal alone one cannot possibly see that its contents embody matters that are spiritual and celestial."

He looks at the entire Bible as a guidebook that tells us about our spiritual journey to the next life. It is full of good advice on how we should live our lives, and the pitfalls we may encounter on the way. Swedenborg writes that the six days of creation correspond to the six stages of our spiritual growth. The seventh day corresponds to heaven.

What about the story of Noah and the ark? Does mankind actually believe that our loving God would kill much of the world's population? He doesn't think so. According to Swedenborg the ark represents the new person we become when we fully rely on the Lord. The animal pairs are the good things we should keep with us. The flood represents the evil that is washed away from our lives. Swedenborg says there is always an inner, spiritual meaning containing deep spiritual wisdom guiding us to our own spiritual growth.

In summary, Swedenborg's theology encompasses the following concepts:

- The Bible is the Word of God; however its true meaning differs greatly from its obvious meaning. Swedenborg via the help of Angels, felt he could shed light on the true meaning of the Scriptures.

- He believes the world of matter is a laboratory for the soul, and that the material is used to refine the spiritual.

- He was universal in his concepts. He believed that all religious systems have their divine duty and purpose, and that this is not only the sole virtue of Christianity.

- He saw the real purpose of Christ's life in the example it gave to others. He vehemently rejected the literal interpretation of the concept of Christian atonement and original sin.

The latter concept is surprising because Swedenborg was the son of a Lutheran minister, and he was raised in an atmosphere full of religion as well as the Bible. Therefore, it is truly amazing that he was so nontraditional. He claims he was in daily contact with the Spirit world, and received much instruction and revelation concerning life after death. He is considered to have made a tremendous impact and contribution to the dispensation of spiritual truth, and has written volumes on spiritual matters. I encourage you to check out his ideas for yourself.[14]

CHAPTER TWENTY-FOUR

Are we now on the road to world peace? There have been several steps taken along this road, which although they have been modest, have been very significant. An uprising began in Tunisia on December 17, 2010, when a college graduate, Mohammed Bonazizi, set himself on fire. Bonazizi was selling vegetables in order to eke out a living for himself. The police confiscated his cart because he had not gotten a license. This dramatic, desperate act inspired thousands of graduates who were also unemployed to take to the streets in protest. There was severe police brutality in the form of arrests, beatings, and murders. The protests continued and spread throughout the country. In the end, on January 14, 2011, the president, Ben Ali, who had been in power for twenty-three years, was forced to flee the country with his family. It is too early to tell whether the interim government will be democratic. But it has shown the Arab dictators that they are not invincible, and it has demonstrated to the Arab people that they have power when they act collectively.

Only weeks later, Egypt's thirty-year-old regime was thrown into havoc by thousands of protesters from all walks of life. They were Muslims and Christians, yuppies and the unemployed. There were people of all ages.

Their feelings of anger had been repressed for years at the hands of President Hosni Mubarek. Some two million protesters were televised in Cairo's Tahrir Square, and there were significant numbers in Alexandria and other cities. During the uprising Cairo, the capital city, was described as a war zone, and there were violent clashes, also, in the port city of Suez. Over 800 people were killed, including at least 135 protesters, and 6000 people were injured.

The grievances focused on legal and political issues including police brutality, state of emergency laws, lack of free elections and freedom of speech, vast corruption, high unemployment, and low minimum wages. On February 11, 2011 Mubarek resigned from office. Two days later the constitution was suspended and both houses of parliament were dissolved. The military was to rule for six months, until elections could be held. However, there are continuing concerns about how long the military junta will actually last. The story is not finished. In the meantime Mubarek has been charged with crimes against his people and is currently standing trial.

Just a few months later, Osama bin Laden, the mastermind behind the worst terrorist attack on American soil, was killed. The raid on his compound in Pakistan was carried out by Navy Seals. His body was buried at sea. President Obama called former President George W. Bush to inform him of bin Laden's death. In his statement Bush said, "The fight against terror goes on, but tonight America has sent an unmistakable message: No matter how long it takes, justice will be done."

And thus, this man who was responsible for the killing of so many innocent people, was taken down, and the families of his many victims could breathe a sigh of relief that he would kill no more.

The question of world peace still has many hurdles to overcome. One of the big problems are the news programs who, night after night, week after week, show stories of violence—rape, murders of innocent people, parents killing their children, etc. Repeatedly the newscasters focus on negative happenings. This makes news! The positive, uplifting events which are taking place worldwide are completely ignored.

In doing research for this book I have come across many positive happenings. I've already mentioned the numerous websites dealing with raised consciousness. In addition to this there are also many websites dealing with interfaith initiatives. I just stumbled across a great one. It is called "United Communities of Spirit."

UCS is a global interfaith network which brings together people of diverse faiths and beliefs who are interested in working with others to build a better world. Their aim is to raise awareness that all humanity is part of the same spiritual family. As of August 2011, UCS had over ten thousand members, from 111 nations, and it encompasses more than three hundred faith groups. It has many interesting and uplifting features, including a volume of World Scriptures which was compiled over five years by forty scholars of various faiths. There is a section in this enormous spiritual work called "The Truth in Many Paths" which quotes from varied sacred scriptures showing their acceptance of one God within their religion.

One example is the Bible: "And Peter opened his mouth and said, 'Truly I perceive that God shows no partiality, but in every nation anyone who fears him and does what is right is acceptable to him'" (Acts 10:34-35).[15]

If you truly long for the coming of World Peace, know that you are not alone. There is strength in numbers. The protesters who took to the streets during the Arab Spring joined thousands of others who shared their dream of freedom, and thus were able to accomplish their goal.

Very recently President Obama said that the biggest threat of terror does not come from organized groups, although of course, they have to be watched very closely, and many of our resources are focused on monitoring them. He felt one of the biggest threats are "lone wolves" who act alone and, therefore, are extremely hard to detect. Apart from those who would murder and maim others in the name of their religion, there are those who are so rigid in their religious beliefs, that they aren't able to accept that religions, other than their own, speak the truth and are trying to lead the way to the Kingdom of God here on earth.

As I was preparing this manuscript I had a brief encounter with such a Christian woman. I excitedly reported my discovery of Emanuel Swedenborg to her, and the spiritual writings he shared with the world. Upon saying he had channeled this knowledge from the Spirit world, she immediately informed me that there are only two sources available. "One is from God, and one is from the Devil!" she proclaimed. And since she didn't believe that Swedenborg's revelations were from God, his beliefs had to have come from the Devil. The look on her face was one of contempt for me. It stopped me in my tracks. First, this righteous lady did not bother to read any of his writings, and obviously, she didn't want to.

How can you determine if someone's writings are from the Devil, if you haven't bothered to read what he has written? Swedenborg was definitely a believer in Christ, but through his experiences formed some of his own beliefs, as I outlined previously. And the look of disapproval that emanated from her face said volumes. If God is the Ultimate source of love, as most religions believe, is this the way to react to something you don't agree with? She could have said she didn't agree with this learned man, but to say he was channeling the

Devil, was very hurtful, because I hold Swedenborg in very high esteem. Unfortunately, if you don't agree with such believers, they feel they have the right to treat you with utter disrespect; because their way is the only right way, or so they think. To be verbally abusive is wrong, and is not a teaching that came from Christ. Thinking your way is the only way is one of the chief roadblocks to peace, and unfortunately, too many people belong in this category.

CHAPTER TWENTY-FIVE

M oving right along, it is clear that, indeed, not all Christians are rigid in their thinking. Many, after doing extensive research, have allowed themselves to think "out of the box." One such person was a Frenchman, born in 1881. His name is Pierre Teilhard de Chardin. He was not only a philosopher and paleontologist, he was also a Jesuit priest. His book *The Phenomenon of Man* was completed in the 1930s, but it was not published until after his death in 1955. The Roman Catholic Church initially prohibited the publication since Teilhard's writing contradicted the church's beliefs.

Teilhard views evolution as a process that leads to increasing complexity for humankind and leads to greater consciousness, a concept that this author has explored previously. He says knowledge accumulates and is transmitted in increasing levels of depth and complexity. This, in turn, leads to a further augmentation of consciousness and the emergence of a "thinking layer that envelopes the earth." Teilhard calls this new membrane the "noosphere." According to Teilhard, "The noosphere is the collective consciousness of humanity, the networks of thought and emotion in which all are involved."[16]

Teilhard goes on to describe a "single organized membrane over the Earth." Many people think that his description which says that all the thinking elements of the earth will find themselves there individually and collectively....clearly relates to the internet, which did not come into existence for another fifty years. Talk about predicting the future!

Teilhard said that as humanity became more self-reflective and able to appreciate its place within space and time, its evolution would begin to move by great leaps rather than by slow movements. We will live in a new type of existence within our full potential. This has been named the "Omega Point."

The reality of our current lives has many people doubting that we are moving toward a marvelous 'omega point' in our destiny. It is believed though that "both spiritual progress and intellectual advancement can exist simultaneously with evil." Teilhard in fact saw things like totalitarianism as a natural part of social evolution, which would be superseded by better forms of organization and community.

Teilhard was a man of great intelligence and an abundance of spirituality. Much of what he foresaw has already come true. Here is an enticing statement he made in *The Phenomenon of Man*: "Everywhere on Earth, at this moment....there floats in a state of extreme mutual sensitivity, love of God and faith in a new world: The two essential components of the ultra-human. These two components are everywhere in the air. Sooner or later there will be a chain reaction."

He goes on to say, "The outcome of the world, the gates of the future, the entry into the super-human—these are not thrown open to a few of the privileged nor to one chosen people to the exclusion of others. They will open only to an advance of all together, in a direction in which all together can join and find completion in a spiritual renovation of the earth."[17]

It is interesting to note that Teilhard lived during the time of Baha'u'llah, who was the founder of Baha'i Faith, since their writings have so many similarities. As mentioned previously, Baha'is believe this was one of the developments of the new age thinking which had been heralded in during this time, and was part of the message which permeated the "noosphere." This term is still being used by leaders of the movement for "raised consciousness."

Baha'u'llah was born in 1817 to one of Persia's best known and wealthiest families. However, he turned his back on his position and announced his support of the Bab (the Gate) who announced to the world that a Messenger of God would soon appear among them. Because of his religious beliefs, the Bab suffered severe persecution at the hands of the Islamic clergy. He was arrested, beaten, and imprisoned. On July 9, 1850, he was executed. His remains are entombed in a beautiful shrine with a golden dome in Haifa, Israel.

Once Baha'u'llah announced his support of the Bab, he also became enmeshed in the wave of violence which was directed to the Bab's followers. Besides losing his worldly endowments, he also was subjected to torture and imprisonment and a series of banishments. While imprisoned in Tehran He had a revelation that He was the One promised by God. This took place in 1852. He was later banished to Baghdad where, in 1865 he publicly revealed this revelation.

Thereafter, he was also sent to Constantinople, Adrianople, and lastly to Acre in the Holy Land. During the latter years of his life he wrote a series of letters to the rulers existing around the world. In these letters he prophesied the coming unification of humanity and the emergence of a world civilization. The rulers he addressed were asked to settle their differences, curtail their armaments, and work toward the establishment of world peace.

In 1892 Baha'u'llah passed away at Bahji, just north of Acre, and he is buried at that site. Now, more than one hundred and fifty years since it was established, the Baha'i Faith, via its members, is striving to create world peace, based on the principles of unity, justice, and continuing advancement.

CHAPTER TWENTY-SIX

❧❧❧

The road to world peace is a steep climb, but with determination many mountains have been climbed throughout history. Much of the history of Mount Sinai took place during biblical times. Mount Sinai is mentioned many times in the Book of Exodus in the Torah and the Bible, and the Quran as well. Moses received the Ten Commandments on this biblical mountain according to Jewish, Christian and Islamic Scriptures.

Here we are in the twenty-first century. How appropriate that the entourage which was the focal point in Redfield's *The Twelfth Insight* was climbing to the top of this very mountain in order to acknowledge and understand the realization of all the spiritual insights outlined in this widely read book. It was believed that once this Ultimate Consciousness was embraced by the majority of mankind, we will have started on the stretch of highway leading to The Most Great Peace, which was foretold by Baha'u'llah.

In my opinion, we are currently on a path to The Lesser Peace, although it is not possible to know how this will enfold in the future. On a global level, we are aware that a multitude of people are rising up and protesting the treatment of unjust rulers who have flourished for many decades in times gone by. This was known as the Arab Spring. Citizens in the Middle East have been willing to give their lives to achieve the freedom and justice which are their due. Some years ago this would have been thought impossible. But as time progresses many things have come about which at one time were considered impossible. The invention of radio, TV, internet, airplanes and space shuttles were at one time believed to be impossible. But all of these things are now in existence.

At this time, the world is currently in transition. Connie Barlow, a noted scientist, talks about evolution in "The Great Story" also known as the "Universe Story." It tells the fourteen billion year science-based story of cosmic genesis. It includes the formation of the galaxies and the origin of earth life. It goes on to the subject of comprehensive compassion, and offers ideas to help humanity in living harmoniously with each other. It is said to enrich the religious experience of all people and all faiths. Thereby, it offers hope for expanded interfaith dialogue and harmony. It is one of many vehicles which can help people come together.

In conclusion, I would like to quote from the Bible. Isaiah 2: 2-4....Let us go up to the mountain of the God of Jacob, and he will teach us of his ways, and we will walk in his path; for out of Zion shall go forth the law, and the word of the Lord from Jerusalem. And he shall judge among the nations, and shall rebuke many people: and they shall beat their swords into plow shears, and their spears into pruning hooks: nation shall not lift up sword against nation, neither shall they learn war anymore."

In April 2011, I became a great-grandmother. The baby boy was given a biblical name: Isaiah. I recently celebrated my eightieth birthday. My hope for little Isaiah is that he will grow up in good health and live to celebrate his eightieth birthday, also. I pray that, at that time, he looks at the condition of the world he lives in, and that he can say to his family gathered around him, "We are at the beginning of The Most Great Peace. Nation shall not lift up sword against nation. Neither shall they learn war anymore."

Amen.

END NOTES

[1] Familydoctor.org editorial staff. "The Exercise Habit." January, 1996. FamilyDoctor.org. December 2010. July 1, 2011
http://familydoctor.org/familydoctor/en/prevention-wellness/exercise-fitness/exercise-basics/the-exercise-habit.html

[2] "Get enough sleep. U matter." June 15, 2011, July 10, 2011.
http://www.umatterucangethelp.com/index.php?option=com_k2&view=itemlist&layout=generic&tag=depression&task=tag

[3] "Live Your Life Well: Help Others," *Mental Health America*, July 11, 2011.
http://www.liveyourlifewell.org/go/live-your-life-well/others

[4] Marilyn Adamson. "Is There a God?" EveryStudent.com. Marilyn Adamson. July 11, 2011.
http://www.everystudent.com/features/isthere.html?

[5] Dr. Elisabeth Kubler-Ross. July 14, 2011.
http://www.near-death.com/experiences/experts02.html

[6] Silver, Brother Larry. *Spiritual Breakfast*. Yellow Springs: Spiritual Identity Ministries, 2010. p. 185

[7] *Aging Health*. "Physical Activity and the Risk of Dementia in Oldest Old." April 2007. National Institute of Health Public Access. Aleksandra Samic, MPH, Yvonne L. Michael S.D, Nicole E. Carlson, PhD, Diane B. Howleson, PhD and Jeffrey A. Kaye,

MD, PhD. June 2011. July 20, 2011.
http://www.ncbi.nlm.nih.gov/pmc/articles/PMC31107
22/

[8] "Suicide in the U.S.: Statistics and Prevention."
National Institute of Mental Health. Sept. 2010. July
20, 2011.
http://www.nimh.nih.gov/health/publications/suicide
-in-the-us-statistics-and-prevention/index.shtml

[9] 65 Club. 08033.com Organizations. John McAdams.
1/19/10. August 2011.
http://209.189.56.28/ORGANIZATIONS.NSF/by+75
+Name/65%20Club?OpenDocument

[10] "Stronger Gun Control Laws." change.org. Wendy
Davis, 2012.
http://www.change.org/petitions/stronger-gun-
control-laws

[11] Congressman Dennis J. Kucinich. "Peace."
February 2009.
http://kuchinich.house.gov/issues/issueID=15647

[12] URI. United Religions Initiative.
http://www.uri.org/

[13] URI. Religions for Peace and Harmony Conference.
April 2011.
http://www.uri.org/the_latest/2011/06/religions_for_p
eace_and_harmony_conference

[14] Rev. Simeon Stefanidakis. "Forerunners to Modern
Spiritualism: Emanuel Swedenborg." "About the First
Spiritual Temple." Rev. Simeon Stefanidakis. 8/1/2011.
http://www.fst.org/spirit2.htm

[15] Origin Research. A Global Interfaith Initiative. January 1996. United Communities of Spirit. Origin Research, October 2011.
http://origin.org/ucs/home.cfm

[16] Matrix Masters. 2000-2003. "The Internet and The Noosphere." Matrix Masters. "The Spirit of the Internet." January 2012.
http://www.matrixmasters.com/spirit/html/2a/2a.html

[17] Pierrre Teilhard de Chardin. *The Phenomenon of Man.* 1955, p. 245

CPSIA information can be obtained
at www.ICGtesting.com
Printed in the USA
FFOW051314260213
926FF